Critical Encounters II

CRITICAL ENCOUNTERS II

Writers and Themes in Science Fiction

Edited by Tom Staicar

FREDERICK UNGAR PUBLISHING CO.   NEW YORK

Copyright © 1982 by Frederick Ungar Publishing Co., Inc.
Printed in the United States of America

Library of Congress Cataloging in Publication Data

Main entry under title:

Critical encounters II.
  (Recognitions)
  Bibliography: p.
  1. Science fiction—History and criticism—
Addresses, essays, lectures.   I. Staicar, Tom.
II. Series.
PN3433.8.C73   809.3'876   82-4838
ISBN 0-8044-2837-9   AACR2
ISBN 0-8044-6876-1 (pbk.)

Contents

Editor's Foreword

You don't have to be a science fiction expert to enjoy this book. People of all ages and from all types of backgrounds are turning to SF in increasing numbers because it provides a fresh way of looking at the challenges we face in the world today. Entertainment and escape are part of the success story of SF, but the genre also provides an opportunity for writers to make statements about science, political theories, and social systems.

Critical Encounters II, like its predecessor, is part of the unique RECOGNITIONS series. Rather than discuss SF in a dry, academic style, our books treat it as a living literature of change and excitement. No background reading is required to get the full value from this book. Whether you are new to science fiction or an aficionado, you will gain new insights about the work of today's finest SF authors as you read the essays in this volume.

These essays were specially written for our collection by people who share a love for science fiction—experts who base their opinions and conclusions on solid research and an extensive knowledge of the field. The subjects of the essays range from the Golden Age pulp magazine writers of the 1940s through the award-winning newcomers of the 1980s and cover diverse and intriguing topics:

Readers of the popular novels of Roger Zelazny might not be aware that he bases much of his work in mythology and symbolism. One of our essays uncovers the roots of Zelazny's writings and explains the hidden meanings found there.

Admirers of Robert A. Heinlein's related "future history" stories (which deal with the progression of future events as if they had already taken place) may not have read anything of the extensive Soviet future history cycle written by the Strugatsky brothers. In their version, now available in English, the United States is *not* a major world power.

How would it feel to be a telepath who finds that he is now losing his powers? That subject is explored in an essay about Robert Silverberg's novel *Dying Inside*.

What would it be like to achieve immortality? Two views of the *unhappy* aspects of living forever are found in Richard Matheson's classics *The Shrinking Man* and *I Am Legend*. Both novels were made into popular films and are the subject of one of our essays.

Could a miscalculation by scientists today cause a future Earth to suffocate from a deadly environment? In *The Nitrogen Fix*, scientist/SF writer Hal Clement describes a world in which we all might live some day, and our essayist explains the background of this novel.

Noted SF historian and scholar Eric S. Rabkin looks at the way science and fiction have come together since Jonathan Swift and Mary Shelley.

These and other topics are presented here in a lively, engaging style. Notes follow the text rather than interrupt the flow of the reading, and brief bibliographies have been added for those readers who wish to pursue subjects further.

Taken as a whole, the range and sheer mass of science fiction may seem overwhelming. More than 1,200 books are published each year bearing the label "SF"; we offer this collection as a guide to some of the most provocative and worthwhile fiction to be found on crowded bookstore shelves. Whether used in a classroom or read for personal pleasure, this book, we are confident, will be an enriching and rewarding experience.

T. S.

Ted Krulik

REACHING FOR IMMORTALITY
Two Novels of Richard Matheson

Many people who are not science fiction aficionados judge the genre by what they see on television and in the movies. For that reason, media people have dubbed the SF films of the 1950s and early 1960s as the period of the bug-eyed monster, or BEM. Unaware that the covers of pulp magazines of the 1920s and 1930s regularly depicted BEMs groping at half-nude females, filmmakers later explained the sudden spate of monsters as the consequence of our newest technological advance on the road to scientific betterment—the atomic bomb.

Among the many movies that enticed audiences with visions of giant insects and mutated beings were two that avoided the cliché of the BEM: *The Last Man on Earth* (1964) and *The Incredible Shrinking Man* (1957). Both of these movies had their genesis in books written by a single author in the 1950s, Richard Matheson. The Vincent Price film *The Last Man on Earth*, later remade with Charlton Heston as *The Omega Man*, was originally entitled *I Am Legend* (1954); *The Incredible Shrinking Man*, prior to its movie release, was simply called *The Shrinking Man* (1956).

Both novels describe the terrible consequences of man-made forces. Instead of the threat of the usual giant insect or mutant, unnatural forces, related to the release of nuclear energy, affect ordinary people and change their environments in drastic ways. These two novels offer a fresh slant to the Things-Better-Left-Untouched motif so often used in science fiction since the dropping of the Hiroshima bomb.

At their core, *I Am Legend* and *The Shrinking Man* take us into the thoughts and feelings of ordinary men struggling to survive in highly unusual circumstances. In *I Am Legend*, Matheson has reworked the last man on earth theme; his protagonist, Robert Neville, is the last living man plagued by an army of the living dead—vampires. Scott Carey, in *The Shrinking Man*, is separated from society by his decreasing size, until he must survive alone in an alien world created by the increasing immensity of the basement in which he is trapped.

Trivial domestic details and descriptions of everyday objects present a clear contrast with the strangeness of the situations in which Neville and Carey find themselves. In *The Shrinking Man*, the increasing size of familiar objects creates a sinister realm that Scott Carey must cope with. Because of his altered sense of scale, an ordinary oil burner becomes a huge thundering tower. The wall beside it appears as an enormous cliff, the strewn sand on the floor is seen as a vast desert, and a common spider seems to be a frightful creature as tall as he is.

Part of the horror that the reader feels about Carey's predicament is in the fact that he no longer has control over the paraphernalia that people take for granted. The familiar has become a terrible, unknown frontier; at the same time, there is a fascination about the threats that might lurk in such a minuscule world.

In *I Am Legend*, an attention to domestic details forms an ironic comparison with Robert Neville's situation. Contrasted with the daily routines of making a life for himself are Neville's supernatural preparations. While he carefully washes his hands and makes sandwiches and coffee for a seemingly pleasant little trek, he also sharpens stakes and carries them in a bag like a latter-day Van Helsing, to be used in the well-known way against vampires.

An integral part of the dream of being the last person on earth is the freedom to roam anywhere one wants, to enjoy all the fruits of civilization left to him. Significantly, such a fantasy has the bonus of freedom from the responsibilities we all face in tending to a job, a home, automobile, family, and the other activities that whirl around our lives. In the world of Robert Neville, we see this fantasy come to life. All the fruits of modern technology lie before him, for his use alone. He has no responsibilities to any other people. His only responsibility is to himself, to maintain a comfortable existence, and to assure his own survival.

Matheson reveals a belief that living in an unknown frontier can be beneficial to man. Natural self-reliance in facing a wilderness is missing from our machine-age existence. As horrible as Scott Carey's life in *The Shrinking Man* has become in his cellar world, he philosophically reflects on his condition:

> He stared a while longer at his face. It was unusually calm for the face of a man who lived each day with dread and peril. Perhaps jungle life, despite physical danger, was a relaxing one. Surely it was free of the petty grievances, the disparate values of society. It was simple, devoid of artifice and ulcer-burning pressures. Responsibility in the jungle world was pared to the bone of basic survival. There were no political connivings necessary, no financial arenas to struggle in, no nerve-knotting races for superior rungs on the social ladder. There was only to be or not to be.

Thus, we see a common bond between Matheson's protagonists. Carey and Neville are representative of the frontier spirit, seeking survival in the face of cruel hardships.

The lengthy, mundane descriptions of Neville's daily life in *I Am Legend* might seem tiresome to the reader, but they vividly illustrate what we would have to go through if we had to rebuild civilization around our needs. (Perhaps the author assumed that nearly everyone has dreamed of being the only human survivor, free to wander among the spoils of civilization.) But Matheson doesn't leave it at that; he instills a nightmare aspect into this fantasy of our childhood—other beings out there, trying to get at and kill the protagonist. With its step-by-step description of Neville's actions, *I Am Legend* breathes realism into everyman's nightmare of being chased and almost caught by creatures from beyond the grave. As night falls, Neville must hit and shove and scratch his way back into his house when he realizes he had been outside too long. Using all his strength, he closes the front door on the arm of one vampire, crushing it until it is broken and useless. Then Neville pushes the limb back out and locks the door.

The reader feels a catharsis with Neville's success at warding off the vampires' attacks. In a violent world, Neville has the strength to meet violence with violence. With his stoic, self-reliant way of life and his dynamic physical struggle against the vampires, he is a hero we can admire.

For Scott Carey, however, an important part of his problem is concerned with failing strength and failing masculinity as he shrinks. He can't simply punch his way out of his predicament the way Robert Neville could. He is fighting his own feelings of weakness and loss in addition to any real enemy. This loss of strength is in part the reason why he becomes trapped in the cellar in the first place; he fights a losing battle with a creature that, under normal conditions, he would have nothing to fear from. A bird twice his size forces Carey against the cellar window when he inadvertently finds himself locked out of his house. Using snow from the ground, Carey tries to chase off the attacking bird, but to little avail. He doesn't have the strength or forcefulness that Neville has. As a result, Carey is beaten back and falls into the cellar, from which he finds no escape. In counterpoint to the fantastic situation, a tiny man fending off an ordinary bird, is the realism of the scene, expressed through selected details of the exterior of the house, the cellar window, and the snow.

A significant reason why both of Matheson's novels read with a down-to-earth realism is because his descriptions are taken right from life. Those scenes of hardship and survival in the cellar of Carey's home obtain their power of empathy because Matheson was there. In a recent interview, Matheson explained:

> You cannot take away your life from your writing, no matter how you try to disguise it. When I wrote *The Shrinking Man*, we were living in a little house on Long Island. I would go down to the cellar every day to write, and would make the cellar in the story exactly the same.

Although author Damon Knight seemed to frown on Matheson's homespun technique when he wrote: "He has a profound interest in the trivia of his daily life," it is Matheson's ability to capture a sense of realism in a few lines of scenery which allows the reader to take the imaginative leap necessary. The author's detailed method makes plausible the nightmare thoughts that many people share, at least as children. The process of seeking some credible scientific excuse for the mythologies and superstitions of the human imagination is an important part of Matheson's writings. If vampires really could exist, how could they be explained? If shrinking were a genuine possibility, how could science explain the phenomenon? Can the workings of fantasy be explained in rational terms? Another author could have shrouded the causes of vampirism or shrinking in mystery, or made veiled implications about their conditions. But Matheson, much to his credit, presents the science behind the fantasy.

In *I Am Legend*, the reader learns with Neville that the vampire state develops from a germ like any other disease. With his discovery of the *bacillus vampiris* on a microscope, Neville wipes away all the superstitious fears of centuries. Although Matheson's pseudoscientific explanations may not stand up to informed scrutiny, it is remarkable how much his bacillus can explain. In one part, Neville tells another normal human how a stake kills a vampire without the need to be driven through the heart. He explains that the bacillus supplies energy to the "undead" as long as it is not exposed to oxygen. If, however, the germ is exposed, it becomes parasitic and feeds upon the body that had acted as its host. Thus, any deep wound in the body, no matter where, allows air in, and the vampire is destroyed. Even if this seems like pseudoscientific gibberish, we can enjoy digesting this highly interpretive theory that rationalizes the existence of the vampire.

Matheson uses similar medical terminology to describe the reasons for Scott Carey's condition in *The Shrinking Man*. The immediate biological cause of his shrinking is an irreversible and persistent loss of specific bodily elements, such as nitrogen, creatinine, phosphorus, and calcium; these elements are associated with development of tissue and muscle, and bone. Matheson is attempting to deal with one of the basic considerations of the SF genre, the "what if—" question. What if a person could shrink? How might it happen? What experiences might he have? By using medical jargon that sounds half-reasonable to answer some of these questions, the author shows a high regard for the science behind the unknown.

Damon Knight points out a serious problem in the construction of *The Shrinking Man*. Matheson's story is inconsistent in its showing of Carey's weaknesses and physical incapabilities. Knight's argument is that Carey should not have been shown struggling hard to lift large objects and scale mountainous terrains if, at the end of the novel, he discovers that a fall of hundreds of feet leaves him unhurt. An explanation comes to mind, but it is not based on any scientific rationale. It was important for dramatic effect, for keeping in character with the failing strength of Scott Carey, that he struggle for each small gain in his basement world. Matheson's motivation for showing Carey surviving a fall that should have killed him had nothing to do with scientific accuracy or relative stresses in differing molecular densities. Carey's survival from that great fall illustrated that he was no longer part of the human race in any physical sense. His physical being had finally taken on all the attributes of an insect, not just in size. His world had become an alien realm beyond our experience.

A serious concern that Matheson shared with many SF writers in the post-nuclear bomb era was the consequence on human beings of such tremendous energy unleashed. The blame for Scott Carey's shrinking and the creation of vampires, as well as the end of the world that Robert Neville knows, falls on the maladjustment of our world to the use of atomic power.

In the 1950s, the probability of man-made forces changing the lives of all human beings was a real fear. Many viewed Soviet communism as a presence that threatened all of our lives. The paranoia of the 1950s was based on the collective thought that some half-crazed official at the Kremlin might push the button that would instigate a world holocaust.

In *The Shrinking Man*, the cause of Carey's problem is a combination of man-made factors, including atomic radiation. But it was not the result of any single, deliberate act. It had been a random accident, a case of being in the wrong place at the wrong time that could never be repeated in a million tries. The alteration in Carey's body occurred when he was subjected to a mist of radiation shortly after getting a large dose of insect spray. Its effect on him could only happen with "just that amount of insecticide coupled with just that amount of radiation, received by his system in just that sequence and with just that timing."

In *I Am Legend*, the cause of the world-wide plague seems clear and direct. The world that Neville comes from casually accepts the dropping of atomic bombs, perhaps in some limited nuclear attack. Neville and his wife matter-of-factly discuss the effects, dust storms and mosquitoes that spread disease. During the time when Neville ekes out his existence in a dead world, it seems that the mosquitoes and the vampires have inherited the earth.

Matheson's use of science is a means to an end; it brings realism to the predicament of his characters. That realism helps the reader to identify with Neville and Carey. To Matheson, scientific advance can be a dangerous thing to the individual. His people have simple, domestic worries and share genuine feelings with us; science is a disruptive force that is capable of ripping such a person from all that he knows.

The "Fishbowl Effect" is my way of explaining what science fiction does. If one imagines oneself in the frame of reference of a goldfish in a fishbowl, one will view that fishbowl as his world, his universe. When the fish is given special adaptations so that it can be removed from its fishbowl, it will perceive the limitations of what it had once thought was the entire world. It will have a drastically new perspective about its former world and, being an outsider to our society, offer us fresh and unique views about ourselves. Many science fiction stories cause this "Fishbowl Effect" to happen to their protagonists—in fact, nearly all fiction portrays characters changing after gaining new perspectives—and also affects readers in much the same way. We see this in *The Shrinking Man* and, to a lesser extent, in *I Am Legend*.

Robert Neville shares the gain of a new insight almost directly with the reader. He changes our view of the sinister presence of the dead-returned-to-life through his discovery of a scientific reason for vampirism. The vampire is no longer a creature of mystery and mystical powers; here is a science that explains the reason for a vampire's existence and all the myths surrounding our understanding of them. The reader finds a new way of looking at all superstitious fears, not only of the vampire. By making the vampire a known quantity, with a scientific basis, Robert Neville gives us a reason to reflect that the unknown need not be fearful.

Neville's realization at the end of the novel that he is the one who is different from the others gives the reader a new slant on the makings of civilization. The reader, like Neville, always had assumed that a truly civilized society sought to better itself, removing the undesirable elements and improving on the better qualities of people and the community. In essence, society encourages health, strength, and achievement, while hoping to eliminate disease, poverty, and criminality. When we learn that a new civilization is in the developing stages, one that is infected with the sickness that caused the world-wide death and creation of vampires, a new civilization that is seeking to destroy all the remnants of past human society, our assumptions are shaken. Robert Neville is the last of his kind, the last of our kind; a new form of homo sapiens is inheriting the earth. What the new race will do with their civilization and what they will think of ours are implications which alter our perspective about our own way of life and what future generations might think of us.

In a jarring moment, Scott Carey in *The Shrinking Man*, trapped in his basement, is thrust into a radically distorted perspective of his former world. As he walks toward his shelter under the water heater, a thunderous noise disrupts the cellar world. A huge, other-worldly figure looms over him, shaking his minuscule world with shoes several times his own height. Some new understandings strike Carey simultaneously: the new shock that the cellar realm he accepted can be disturbed by the life "out there;" the vision of a person the size that he once was; and the realization that this monstrosity with elephantine dimensions was once his wife, Louise.

When Carey wonders afterward why he didn't try to call to her, he realizes that he no longer has any relationship to his wife, or to the world he once knew. The reader understands that there is no way for Carey to go back, that he does not belong in that world. In an almost literal way, Scott Carey is a fish abruptly taken out of his fishbowl. While he is still able to view his old way of life, he becomes aware that he must forge a new one.

In his first weeks of shrinking, Carey confronted a basic truth about human nature. It can be expressed by his thought: "Poets and philosophers could talk all they wanted to about a man's being more than fleshly form, about his essential worth, about the immeasurable stature of his soul. It was rubbish." So much of our relationships with other people depend on our physical presence, on what we are, measured in feet and inches, in comparison with others around us.

At thirty-five inches tall, Carey learned this truth of human nature in a bitter confrontation with three young teenagers. Lacking the strength to fight them off while he was walking alone, Carey had to pretend to be a child, feeling his humiliation as he desperately tried to escape them. When the youths recognized him as the shrinking man, their taunting remarks and vicious beating became all the greater because of his attempt to fool them. Although he promised himself at their initial approach that "he'd never be small enough to run from three boys," in the end he ran for his life. Later, when he was certain he had lost them, feeling utterly hopeless and degraded, he began to cry. "It was not a man's crying, not a man's despairing sobs. It was a little boy sitting there in the cold, wet darkness, hurt and frightened."

In another incident, his lessening height affected the aura of respect he had established as a father with his young daughter. Because he was no longer bigger, stronger, more deeply-voiced, he could no longer command authority over his little girl:

> The authority of fatherhood, he discovered, depended greatly on simple physical difference. A father, to his child, was big and strong; he was all-powerful. A child saw simply. It respected size and depth of voice. What physically overshadowed it, it almost always respected or at least feared. Not that Scott had gained Beth's respect by trying to make her fear him. It was simply a basic state that existed because he was six feet two and she was four feet one. . . .

> She could not understand or appreciate. She was not old enough to sympathize. She could only see him baldly. And in the actuality of pure sight, he was nothing but a horrid midget who screamed and ranted in a funny voice. To her he had stopped being a father and had become an oddity.

So Carey learns the truth of a man's worth. And the reader, too, shares the newness of these experiences. Matheson hits home with the realization that it is human nature to view short people as weaker people, with less authority over others. We see the universality in such experiences as related above and can say, Yes, that is the way it could happen, that is the way others would see us if we were shrinking in the same fashion. In moments such as those described, we see the fishbowl of what we were, and can view what we are becoming.

"Why not go out?" It is a question that occurs for both Carey and Neville. For Carey, soon to disappear from the world of humanity, letting the spider catch him was all that was needed. "It would be a hideous death, but it would be quick; despair would be ended." Robert Neville need only heed the call of the vampires for all his problems to be resolved. "Why go through all this complexity when a flung-open door and a few steps would end it all?" However, Matheson's characters belong to a literary tradition in which the hero must grapple with all obstacles and attempt to endure. Locked helplessly in his home each night, Neville's expression of contempt is typical of the hero: "I'll kill every mother's son of you before I'll give in!"

When the infected people came with guns to break in to Neville's house, he put up a valiant effort to defend his home and himself. Having been forewarned of their coming, his defense seemed as heroic as the men at the battle of the Alamo, who knew death would come at the end. Seriously wounded and taken prisoner, Neville's reasons for not leaving when he had the chance appear flimsy, but are the stuff that makes ordinary men attempt extraordinary actions in the face of the greatest dangers: "I was too used to the . . . the house. It was a habit, just . . . just like the habit of living. I got . . . used to it." Weak from his wounds, Neville refused to accept the reality of his death. "In spite of having walked a tightrope of bare existence across an endless maw of death—in spite of that he couldn't understand it. Personal death still was a thing beyond comprehension." Only when Neville saw the fear on the faces of the infected people, and understood what that fear meant, did he relinquish his hold on life.

Although Scott Carey had more readily accepted the coming of death, he expressed doubts about how that death would take shape: "Like death, his fate was impossible to conceive. No, even worse than death. Death, at least, was a concept; it was a part of life, however strangely unknown. But who had ever shrunk into nothingness?" Throughout the novel, Carey was assailed by doubts about his reason for struggling so hard to survive. Many times the means to end his life were put in his path: jumping off a table top to his death, falling down a bottomless hole he found in the cellar floor, or letting hunger and thirst take their final toll on him. Why go on if he faced nonexistence in a few more days?

The affirmation of a will to live continuously overcame Carey's thoughts of death. It seemed that there might be a purpose to his surviving as far as he had. There were too many coincidences from his past that worked to save him now that he was a fraction of an inch tall in his cellar world. A broken box of crackers, one that he had angrily kicked down the basement when he began shrinking, offered sustenance to him later; a long pole tossed aside gave Carey the means to reach the bread near the spider's web high above him. "All the coincidences that had contributed to his survival seemed to go beyond the limits of probability. This, for instance; this pole thrown here in just this way by his own brother. Was that only chance?"

His resolution to climb the "cliff" was made with this reaffirming of purpose to his life. Carey intended not only to reach the bread he needed for nourishment, but to fulfill his need to kill the spider and have sole domain of his universe:

> He didn't let himself think about the spider. He didn't let himself think about the fact that there were only two days left to him, no matter what he did. He was too absorbed in the small triumphs of conquered detail and in the large triumph of conquered despair to let himself be dragged down again by crushing ultimates.

> That was it, then. The pin spear slung across his back, the cracker crumbs and water-soaked sponge in his robe, the pin hook for climbing.

Carey's battle with the spider was even more exhausting and terrifying than the movie version depicts. His resolve in executing those plans was that of a man no longer concerned with his own imminent death. His victory over this monster of dread and evil was everything. "He could sleep without the box top now, sleep free and at peace. A tired smile eased his stark expression. Yes, it was worth it. Everything seemed worth it now."

Matheson's final point in both novels is bonded by a common theme. In their variant ways, Scott Carey and Robert Neville are able to continue after the end of their existence. The events in *I Am Legend* lead to two important revelations of Neville's. First, he realizes he should have foreseen the development of a race of beings who could be infected by the bacteria but who would not become vampires. He sums up his realization in three words: "Bacteria can mutate."

Neville's second discovery embodies the author's prime motive behind the story's title and presents the ultimate purpose of Neville's life:

> Robert Neville looked out over the new people of the earth. He knew he did not belong to them; he knew that, like the vampires, he was anathema and black terror to be destroyed. And, abruptly, the concept came, amusing to him even in his pain.
>
> A coughing chuckle filled his throat. He turned and leaned against the wall while he swallowed the pills. Full circle, he thought while the final lethargy crept into him limbs. Full circle. A new terror born in death, a new superstition entering the unassailable fortress of forever.
>
> I am legend.

As the last of the human race, Neville realizes, as we do, that a new future race of beings could view us as infamous and the stuff of mystical fears. His death not only has meaning, but the future race will remember him until the end of its time.

The concluding revelation in *The Shrinking Man* closely parallels that of *I Am Legend* in its intention to shock the reader as the protagonist is shocked (or surprised). It also reveals the purpose of Carey's existence, his uniqueness as a thinking creature who is smaller than a mote of dust. Believing that his life had been guided by some cosmic plan, Carey finds himself able to leave the imprisoning cellar through the same window from which he entered, because he is finally small enough.

Unlike the ironic but sad end of Robert Neville, Scott Carey's life holds the promise of continued existence in undreamed-of worlds. On the morning after his shrinking was supposed to take him from the face of the earth, he awoke. "He looked up again at the jagged blue dome. It stretched away for hundreds of yards. It was the bit of sponge he'd worn." His surprise and understanding of the "blue dome" mirrors our own. His revelation, like Neville's, comes after life as we know it has no further meaning.

Throwing aside the artificial measurements of mathematics, Carey understood that nature has no such limitations. "To nature there was no zero. Existence went on in endless cycles. It seemed so simple now. He would never disappear, because there was no point of nonexistence in the universe." With new energy and new joy, Scott Carey ran to face the infinite worlds awaiting him. The last words of the movie version encompassed the full meaning of Carey's story. Amid church music and the ringing of bells, Carey's own voice jubilantly told us: "I still exist!"

The popular appeal of these two novels rests on two qualities of any good work of literature: the universality of their themes, and the strong delineation of the characters and their conflicts. *I Am Legend* and *The Shrinking Man* express the universality of such themes as fear of darkness and the nightmare creatures we all fear it may contain; prejudice against anyone who is different from us, and the converse fear that we may be seen as different from others; and a real concern about changes within ourselves because of the world we have made. The novels are vividly personal because of the myriad particulars of Neville's and Carey's lives that Matheson takes the time to describe. We recognize those particulars because they are so much a part of our own lives. Like them, we all must confront our fears and weaknesses; we must endure beyond our mistakes, our embarrassments, and our personal humiliations. Matheson's characters are multifaceted and given to human frailty. They are like us in their drives and desires and they resemble us in our failures and need for the company of others.

The two novels discussed here are good examples of the genre of science fiction in that they describe ordinary human beings in unusual circumstances, and use the language of science as explanation. But they are more than that. They are worthwhile depictions of human endurance and human cares in a world gone haywire, one that looks very much like ours.

2

Jessica Amanda Salmonson

HERO AS HEDONIST
The Early Novels of Doris Piserchia

Of the many themes of science fiction—xenophobic patriotism, wish-fulfilling heroics, doomsaying polemics, romanticized sexism or racism—the advocacy of hedonism is possibly the least common. This may seem surprising, since the primary function of science fiction is to entertain, and hedonists regard pleasure as the highest form of good. In our Judeo-Christian, superficially puritanical culture, however, there really is no contradiction. It is entirely in keeping with social mores that science fiction warn of Armageddon, though in a strictly entertaining manner.

Although religion per se no longer dominates us as overtly as in previous centuries, the fundamental myths on which our daily lives are built are, in the Western world, largely Judeo-Christian in origin. This causes our writers to imply, almost against their will, that *suffering*, not pleasure, is the highest good. Our cultural subconsciousness is far more likely to believe in this than in hedonism. Indeed, only the Satanists are left to preach hedonism with much fervor, believing as they do that the so-called deadly sins, if practiced strictly, actually cancel each other out (i.e., gluttony is restricted by vanity if, in the throes of a Roman feast, one recalls the preferred beauty of a lithe self), resulting in both a moral and happy life-style.

With the precepts of hedonism relegated largely to gigolos and Satanists, even science fiction writers find themselves unable to give the perspective much credence. Hence the genre's fascination with galactic warfare, holocaust, and other sorts of large-scale tragedies, confronted quite often by anguished, brilliant loners whose work ethic and/or messiah complex and/or sheer egoism compel them to give themselves not to pleasure but to a cause, however unrewarding, unappreciated, difficult, or futile.

Doris Piserchia varies from this norm in that her central characters are often hedonists. A story's suspense is not created by the dangerous environments but by antihedonist antagonists. Sometimes these antagonists are self-serving as in *Spaceling*, trying to make a fortune through dishonesty; sometimes they are self-appointed soul savers as in *Earth Child*, trying to win a convert, as it were. The dangers in the environment are rewarding experiences to the protagonists, but the impinging mores of subtle flagellants create problems for those who would, left to their own devices, be happy wild-children, unassimilated and untortured.

The best example of a hedonistic protagonist is found in *Earth Child*. It is a rich, inventive novel, reminiscent in a woman-positive reverse-of-the-coin manner of Jack Vance's *The Eyes Of The Overworld* or *The Dying Earth*; Piserchia also writes high adventure—a blend of fantasy and science fiction (SF)—with humor and wit. Instead of Cugel the Clever, we have Reee (two syllables) of Earth, bright, coordinated, and brave at times, stupid, awkward, and cowardly at others, adventuresome out of necessity. She is a woman-child whose life we trace from the age of four to the age of fifteen—which takes her several thousand years.

Reee is a vibrant youngster of a sort about whom bold myths are made: the last human resident of Earth, a planet inhospitable to all human life except hers. There exist buglike, beastlike, plantlike, and sentient-elemental monsters, mainly hostile with but one ambiguous exception. Death looms over her head at every moment of her life. But it's home! And Reee is unselfconsciously happy with her life and world.

Martians—the descendants of the last people of Earth—constantly try to rescue her and take her to Mars where it is relatively safe (and oppressive), but she evades them for thousands of years and becomes the mythological last inhabitant in their otherwise unimaginative minds and puritanical, workaholic lives. She survives on a world uninhabitable to humans because of her survival instinct, cleverness, luck, oneness with her environment, and by the Will of Her Protectress. Reee is being kept alive against all odds, revitalized when death is upon her or when her body is severely damaged. She is protected, sheltered, and placed in suspended animation periodically by a green elemental (a substance like water or fire) who calls herself Emeroo. We do not know why Emeroo is so intent on keeping Reee alive until the end of the book, and even then it is subject to interpretation. But we do not need to know more specifically. Emeroo is like the good face of a goddess, and the logic of deities often defies human understanding. The enigma of Emeroo does not have to be resolved to be fascinating.

The dark face of the goddess is Indigo, an expanding ocean of dark blue sentient substance that is slowly eating away the world. Indigo is Reee's sworn enemy, or maybe it is not; it is out to destroy her, but not necessarily; and it might succeed except for what seems to be the intervention of Emeroo who is possibly good and, if not loving, then a good approximation of it. These elementals, though threatening and disconcerting are ultimately not the real threat, as they are natural things. The would-be saviors from Mars are the real foes.

Reee lives for herself, the ultimate hedonist. She refuses to do anything she considers stupid, boring, or otherwise self-destructive, even if (as when she is kidnapped and taken to Mars) she is severely punished for her refusals. She is less influenced by what others do to her than by what she does for herself. If she works at Martian toil, she will only bore herself; but if she is lazy, the Martians will starve, ignore, and maybe try to kill her. It does not matter. It is better to risk (and battle) destruction from outside sources than to succumb to self-destruction. Compromise is unacceptable. Self is important. Reee is a heroine.

Jade of *Star Rider* parallels Reee in many ways. Reee rides a gigantic bird named Belios. Jade rides a large, sentient dog named Hinky, who can leap through dimensions from planet to planet when joined with a "jak" (a race of creatures who ride on others). The two animals have no similarities—Belios being a cussed critter who loves Reee in spite of itself, and Hinky being a sweet, protective pup who dotes on his mistress entirely. Yet the "young woman with pet to ride" creates a superficial resemblance between these two marvelous novels. (In a later novel, not discussed in this essay, the hedonistic young protagonist is capable of becoming the animal, eliminating the need of a mount.)

There are other similarities between *Star Rider* and *Earth Child*. Jade is captured and taken to Gibraltar and forced into many of the same situations as Reee was on Mars; both have to deal with people attempting to force them into conformity. Both are tall, strong, young women, whose keepers are at once in awe and contemptuous of them. Both have appetites that startle their captors. Both are hounded by enemies, and both discover that at least one of their enemies is not all bad. And fundamentally, Jade, like Reee, is hedonistic.

There the similarities end. Whereas Reee seems to exist largely to fulfill the needs of Emeroo and Indigo, Jade fulfills only herself. Whereas Reee is protected by an elemental, Jade has power in herself, enough to save all her jak race without having to try. And where Reee's goal is almost mystical, Jade's is merely the pot of gold at the end of the rainbow: Doubleluck, the mythic planet for which all the star-riding jaks are searching. Reee's hedonism becomes a tool by which Emeroo will defeat, or rejoin, her "sister" Indigo. Jade's hedonism takes her to personal glory. That it saves the rest of the galaxy is incidental to her own fulfillment.

Unlike the protagonists of later novels, Daniel Jordan of *Mister Justice* is not allowed to exhibit or experience hedonism. His attitudes are shaped by others so that his genius will be directed toward killing Mr. Justice, a time-hopping vigilante whom the government does not want playing judge and jury regardless of justifications. To the public, Mr. Justice is the ultimate hero. To criminals, he is the wrath of god. To various vindictive, patriotic, or self-serving individuals, he is the "man to beat." To idealistic Daniel, Mr. Justice is superman; and it is disturbing to realize it is himself, a fourteen-year-old boy, who must prepare for the future confrontation that will destroy superman.

Daniel becomes obsessed with his paradoxical destiny—to kill the evil that kills evil. Yet Daniel's natural inclinations are toward hedonism, however unfulfilled. He would "rather wade in mud puddles than collect facts." One character calls Daniel a hedonist to his face, and Daniel retorts, "Damn right." He would run away with his fellow genius Pala, a Swiss girl, and live happily ever after, the hell with destiny, but she is taken away from him by manipulative guardians. He replaces her with his obsession. He will try, after all, to destroy Mr. Justice. He will do nothing else with his life. Even when it is clear that there is greater danger abroad, he will not waver.

There seems to be a message here, something more subtle than the pros and cons of vigilantism—a suggestion that there are only two choices in life, hedonism or folly. Daniel, denied his natural inclinations, forced to bear unreasonable responsibility, becomes as crazy as everybody else. Heroism dies if hedonism cannot prevail.

Humor is always evident in the writings of Piserchia, violent humor, and in *The Billion Days of Earth* it takes its darkest form. Humankind has evolved into veritable gods, and rats have evolved into the ecological niche vacated by Homo sapiens (they might correctly be called Homo rattis). They worship the gods without respect. In turn, the gods are self-centered and careless of the new "men." Other animals have evolved intellects of some degree, though there is minimal contact between species, and compared to *rattis*, other species are moronic.

The Billion Days of Earth and *Mister Justice* have less to do with women than either of the other two books discussed. The major women in these books are Aril, the wife of the protagonist (she is a madwoman, offspring of the inbred upper classes, insanely attached to her monster son) and the goddess Vennavora. Vennavora is an intriguing character who, in the manner of her deity race, can drop out of the sky at any moment to talk to the main characters. It is tempting to think this is Piserchia herself, giving little warnings to her characters, visiting them, and giving the novel its final lament.

The plot is intriguing, complex, and bizarre. The Fillies, or upper class, rule the world. They have inbred for centuries and are doomed to extinction. Their monster children are orphaned to mix with commoners and to ruin the bloodlines of the common folk. The new race of rat-men aspires, like the previous race of monkey-men, to become gods. But the blood of the Fillies hinders the evolutionary process. The novel is full of paranoia and conspiracy and comments almost inadvertently on class oppression.

Rat-men and women have no hands or fingers. They wear metal hands made by a Filly-owned industry. The protagonist, Rik, believes the only difference between himself and the gods is the years of evolution—and since he is one of the rare rat-men with fingers (which he hides in gloves so as not to frighten superstitious people who might take him for one of the increasing number of monsters born each year), he believes he is already on the way to catching up with the gods.

Sheen is an elemental intelligence reminiscent of Emeroo in *Earth Child.* He/it appears as a shapeless mercurylike substance, and proceeds to trick various sentient beings into giving up their egos. Sheen believes himself omniscient, and the fact that he cannot yet absorb the vast egos of the gods is a thorn in his side. That there are certain rat-men who ignore him infuriates, yet humors, him, and he plays elaborate games with the protagonist and his messianic friend, Jak, hoping eventually to convince them to give up their egos and find perfect bliss. Jak, almost a Jesus Christ figure, may or may not be named "Jak"— like the race in *Star Riders*—by coincidence. It could be that the race we see in the later book is descended not of humans but of these rat-men; but there is no other evidence that Piserchia intended any connection between the varied worlds she created.

Sheen is paranoid, somehow knowing that he is not as omniscient as he wants to believe, that he was, like everything else, born of Earth. He considers the possibility that he was "sent" by Mother Earth to purge the face of the globe of the foul stink of evolution gone awry. When the deity race itself becomes threatened by him and leaves for the stars, it is not so much the literal threat of Sheen they resent, but the great Mother Earth who turned against her children. Sheen is not asked his opinion, which must have been the biggest blow to his ego. He was frustrated enough that they left before he was strong enough to eat them; but that they should blame her and not him for their retreat would cut deep into the psyche of this ego-eater.

Although Sheen appears undefeatable, there is some hope suggested in the book. A few will escape his touch and regain their egos; some will never give their egos to him in the first place. The result will be a few particularly worthwhile rat-people who are the cream of the crop, carrying on the evolutionary scheme to a different and better conclusion than Homo superior found. Or—we never learn for certain—the Homo rattis species may never do better. (Unless the destiny of the jaks in *Star Rider* is indeed the direction of evolution for Homo rattis.)

Hedonism plays a smaller role in this novel than in any other, including Piserchia's later works. Neither Jak nor Rik are hedonistic, both having ideals or loves that override their sense of self. The gods may be hedonistic, but more likely they are simply great egotists, which is what makes them attractive to the ego-eater. Sheen may be somewhat hedonistic, yet even he gets his self-esteem by interacting with beings outside himself, and he is bothered about what may become of him when there are no longer egos to devour.

If it is a book without hedonists, however, it is also a book without heros. It may be that there will be a heroic hedonist among the next generation, after both the gods and Sheen are of no importance and when the degenerate Fillies are gone. If there are "messages" in this book, though, they are couched in such grim humor that they are neither obvious nor obtrusive. The novel is frustrating in some places, too whimsical in others, but overall it is unique among Piserchia's first four works—a rogue novel.

That Piserchia means to advocate hedonism is something only she can say; probably she means only to tell a rousing tale, and the underlying themes are as unconscious as those of any writer. The analysis of her first four novels does suggest very strongly that she does not consider the workaholic, the idealist, the obsessive, the messianic, the conformist, or even the intellectual to be as lovably heroic as the hedonist. Daniel of *Mister Justice*, denied his hedonistic tendencies, urged us to pity. Rik and Jak of *The Billion Days of Earth* seem caught up in an inexorable mess that they may survive but cannot influence—they are not the least heroic in either the classical suffering sense or the hedonistic sense. Only Jade of *Star Rider* and Reee of *Earth Child* win our heartfelt approval, love, and applause. Although eschewing creature comforts (themselves a burden), they are yet hedonic in approach, considering no one before themselves, but meaning no one harm if left to their own device of adventuresome pleasure.

3

Eric S. Rabkin

THE RHETORIC OF
SCIENCE IN FICTION

In the physiology section of Wil Huygen and Rien Poortvliet's delightful *Gnomes* (1976), we find the following under the rubric of "Hormones and Sex Organs":

> Research in this area was difficult. In the literature everyone remains silent on the subject. As well as ordinary adrenaline in the blood, gnomes have a type of super-adrenaline that makes for high-level performance in matters involving strength, stamina, and sexual drive. The sex organs are similar in form to those of the human. The female ovulates only once in her life. Exactly how that works, we do not know—but it probably became the norm through some magical intervention about 1,500 years ago. The male remains potent until about 350 years of age.

This passage flies the flags of modern science. We spot code words indigenous to science like "research" and "adrenaline." Other words like "ovulate" and "sex organs" seem to imply a scientific mind that chose them from myriad other possibilities, like "ripen" and "womb." The passage purports to convey incontrovertible information, knowledge, and to that extent it masquerades as part of science itself, the very word *science* deriving from the Latin *scire*, to know. To begin a discussion of the rhetoric of science in fiction, we will need to take up the traditional argument that science is a particular sort of knowledge with necessary relationships to other sorts of knowledge.

But science is not merely, or sometimes even, knowledge. There are no gnomes, I think. I use that fact to recognize this passage as a masquerade. The conflict between science and magic, played here as the conflict between the rhetoric of science and the rhetoric of magic, lends the whole mock-serious paragraph a winning whimsy, the source of which is clearest when a scientific fact is said to derive from "magical intervention." Although science itself may be based on and may institutionalize a certain sort of naturalistic knowledge, the crucial point here is that science has forged for itself a rhetoric that can function even when no claims for real-world truth are being made. Quite the contrary, the rhetoric may be most effective from the artist's point of view precisely because its promise of verifiable knowledge is flaunted. This essay must take account of science, to be sure, but the argument aims not at science itself but at the development and uses of the rhetoric of science.

As readers, we are all aware, even if sometimes only unconsciously, of the rhetorical conflicts that may arise in literature when science is the subject. "In a general way," Max I. Baym writes in the *Princeton Encyclopedia of Poetry and Poetics*:

> ... the relation between science and poetry has had its critics since Plato's suggestion in *The Republic* that there may be a fundamental opposition between the aims of the poet and those of the philosopher.

Although the long history of that conflict needs examination, we may still find profit in the more limited segment of history running from Francis Bacon (1561–1626) to the present, the period in which what we think of as modern science has had acknowledged importance. Focusing on that period, Baym sets forth the orthodox critical view:

> The chief concern from the 17th century down to our present day has been the mind's tilting with a pervasive dualism which would keep poetry and science apart as two antithetical activities of mental operation.

Earl Miner has explored these "activities of mental operation" in a useful and provocative article on "Literature as Knowledge":

> ... we trust the arts to differ from science ... in their kind of relation to truth, that is, in their status as knowledge. ... A poem

or dance does not propose, does not predict. No evidence can be found to verify a pastoral elegy, a still life, or a waltz. . . . Of course poems may use such things as scientific propositions—pre-"Copernican" astronomy for example—that are later falsified. But the virtual status of such an element in a poem saves it from falsification.

Miner speaks with the majority voice in positing the ontological antagonism between science and art, and he is doubtless correct in suggesting that later falsification of a mode of astronomy will not invalidate—or falsify—the poem that happens to use it.

We need to add, however, that a modern poem might also use an outmoded form of astronomy, and use it for its own rhetorical effect. By giving Mars a breathable atmosphere in his 1950 composite novel *The Martian Chronicles*, Ray Bradbury announces that his work is not to be taken entirely as science fiction—and held exclusively to that genre's aesthetic criteria—but rather is to be read at least in part as a kind of fairy tale set in a realm miraculously hospitable to humanity. The falsification of scientific theories and ideas does indeed take place outside fiction. But the knowledge which is produced by that on-going process participates in our reading—and in artists' creating—through our historical understanding of the precise ways in which the world outside the text was thought to exist, including ways determined by science. In this sense, despite the antagonism many people see between science and poetry, science can be, and nowadays frequently is, brought into the service of poetry. Conversely, there is an important body of literature quickly accumulating that argues powerfully for the importance of the intuitive, artistic imagination for the evolution of science. Although much has rightly been made of a post-Renaissance repulsion between science and art, there is no doubt that in the development of science and art, each has helped the other.

When writing "On Fairy Stories" (1938), J. R. R. Tolkien calls the settings of those tales "Faërie," a term which:

> . . . may perhaps most nearly be translated by Magic—but it is magic of a peculiar mood and power, at the furthest pole from the vulgar devices of the laborious, scientific magician.

The antagonism between science and magic is felt as strongly as that between science and art, a feeling indeed which must be

relied upon if Huygen and Poortvliet are to create the delight
they apparently intend. Tolkien's own magic, as is well known,
is Christian, committed magic. The antagonism of science to
religion is for many a matter of faith. Voltaire makes this explicit
in the article on "Common Sense" in his *Philosophical Dictionary* (1764):

> But where does this expression "common sense" come from, if
> not from the senses? When men invented this phrase, they con-
> fessed that nothing entered the mind except by the senses; oth-
> erwise would they have employed the word *sense* to mean com-
> mon reasoning?
>
> People sometimes say: "Common Sense is very rare"; what
> does the phrase mean? That in some men elementary reason was
> arrested in its progress by some prejudices that such a man, who
> judges very sensibly in one matter, will always grossly deceive
> himself in another. Here's an Arab, who is in other respects a good
> calculator, a learned chemist, and a precise astronomer, who
> nevertheless believes that Mahomet has half the moon in his
> sleeve.
>
> Why should he go beyond common sense in the three sciences
> I have mentioned, and fall below it when it comes to that half-
> moon? Because in the first cases he saw with his eyes, he culti-
> vated his intelligence; and in the second he saw with the eyes of
> others, he closed his own, he perverted the common sense within
> him.

This seeing with the eyes of others is the "Idol of the Tribe,"
one of four false idols Bacon names in the *Novum Organum*
(1620) and blames for blinding people to a true understanding
of their world.

For us, Voltaire's opposition of knowledge based on the senses, on calculation, on experimentation, and on observation to
knowledge based on the word of others may seem entirely valid.
Indeed, the rhetoric of science is used precisely against the rhetoric of religion for many purposes, including even mutual satire.
In *Erewhon* (1872), Samuel Butler says that:

> It is only the very great and good who have any living faith in the
> simplest axioms; and there are few who are so holy as to feel that
> 19 and 13 make 32 as certainly as 2 and 2 make 4.

Yet Butler, in his rhetoric, frequently adopts the prevailing common sense of his time, science. Notice how this description from the same book uses calculation, observation, and theoretical inquiry:

> The weather was delightfully warm, considering that the valley in which we were encamped must have been at least two thousand feet above the level of the sea. The river-bed was here about a mile and a half broad and entirely covered with shingle over which the river ran in many winding channels, looking, when seen from above, like a tangled skein of ribbon, and glistening in the sun. We knew that it was liable to very sudden and heavy freshets; but even had we not known it, we could have seen it by the snags of trees, which must have been carried long distances, and by the mass of vegetable and mineral *débris* which was banked against tbeir lower side, showing that at times the whole river-bed must be covered with a roaring torrent many feet in depth and of ungovernable fury.

Butler goes on for two more pages in this vein. Clearly, although the conflicts between science and magic, religion, and art *may* be felt to be inevitable, the rhetorical practices of artists show us that these conflicts are sometimes nonexistent. When the conflict arises, as in Butler's aphorism, we sense the imposition of the mechanic (scientific, calculable, inhuman) on the organic (emotional, elusive, human), we sense, in short, what Henri Bergson, in *Le Rire* (1900) identifies as the universal source of humor. But this imposition is obviously not inevitable, not a matter of the immutable ontology of science and other subjects, but a matter of our views of those subjects and how they function in our lives, views that can be changed even within a single text by the author's manipulation of rhetoric.

Francis Bacon does not see an opposition between science and religion. In fact, Bacon finds the authority for "effecting all things possible," for pursuing the science of *New Atlantis* (1627), in the service science performs for religion. The body of scientists who rule this quasi-Platonic utopia "is dedicated to the study of the Works and Creatures of God . . . [and] is sometimes called Salomon's House and sometimes the College of the Six Days Works." For Bacon, as for anyone committed to the significance of The Book of Genesis, science is inextricably involved with the story of the access of knowledge and the consequent fall into shame, death, childbirth and toil. The loss of Eden lies behind Bacon's assertion in *Novum Organum* that:

> Let but mankind recover their right over nature, which was given them by the Divine Being, let them be well provided of materials, and rectified reason and sound religion will direct the use.

Bacon makes clearest his sense that science is ordained to restore Man's lost dominion by his lengthy catalog in *New Atlantis* of the achievements of Atlantian science. Among these are:

> ... a number of artificial wells and fountains, made in imitation of the natural sources and baths, as tincted upon vitriol, sulphur, steel, brass, lead, nitre, and other minerals. And again we have little wells for infusions of many things, where the waters take the virtue quicker and better than in vessels or basons. And amongst them we have a water which we call Water of Paradise, being, by that we do to it, made very sovereign for health and prolongation of life.

Paradise is another name for Eden, and for Bacon science builds the road back.

Although Bacon saw no ontological conflict between science and religion, he did recognize that the rhetoric of science was crucially different from the rhetoric of religion:

> There are and can be only two ways of searching into and discovering truth. The one flies from the senses and particulars to the most general axioms, and from these principles, the truth of which it takes for settled and immovable, proceeds to judgment and to the discovery of middle axioms. And this way is now in fashion. The other derives axioms from the senses and particulars, rising by a gradual and unbroken ascent, so that it arrives at the most general axioms last of all. This is the true way, but as yet untried.

Nowadays we may sometimes take the opposition between arguments from principles and arguments from particulars as somewhat less antagonistic than did Bacon. All arguments, after all, use both principles and particulars. Yet the effort Bacon was urging, the replacement of a priori argument with appeals to the senses, calculation, observation, and experimentation, intended nothing less than a revolution in habits of mind, habits instituted by rhetoric.

Sidney Warhaft, in the Introduction to his edition of Bacon's works, shows us the "fashion" that Bacon sought to revise by quoting a "respectable" argument motivated by and advanced against Galileo's 1610 report of the telescopic discovery of four moons of Jupiter:

> There are seven windows given to animals in the domicile of the head, through which the air is admitted to the tabernacle of the body, to enlighten, to warm, and to nourish it. What are these parts of the *microcosmos*? Two nostrils, two eyes, two ears, and a mouth. So in the heavens, as in a *macrocosmos*, there are two favourable stars, two unpropitious, two luminaries, and Mercury undecided and indifferent. From this and many other similarities in nature, such as the seven metals, etc., which it were tedious to enumerate, we gather that the number of the planets is necessarily seven. Moreover, these satellites of Jupiter are invisible to the naked eye, and therefore would be useless, and therefore do not exist. Now, if we increase the number of the planets, this whole and beautiful system falls to the ground.

As Miner writes, the falsification of an astronomical system does not falsify literary works, like *The Divine Comedy* (1321), that may depend upon it. Nonetheless it might seem true that an argument like that offered against Galileo would be impossible today. Putting aside the content of the argument, the very beliefs we have about evidence—and hence the right mode of presenting evidence, that is, appropriate rhetoric—are so vastly different from those of the early seventeenth century that we find this "refutation" both quaint and laughable. Yet through these centuries of science, the fashion of arguing from first principles has had a peculiar persistence:

> All these things being consider'd, it seems probable to me, that God in the Beginning, form'd Matter in solid, massy, hard, impenetrable, moveable Particles, of such Sizes and Figures, and

with such other Properties, and in such Proportion to Space, as most conduced to the End for which he form'd them. . . . And therefore that Nature may be lasting, the Changes of Corporeal Things are to be placed only in the various Separations and new Associations and Motions of these permanent Particles.

This early eighteenth century argument from first principles intended to show that light must be thought of as composed of particles and not of waves. The author of this argument was Sir Isaac Newton, arguably one of the foremost scientific minds in the history of our species. One might suggest, of course, that this great empiricist was arguing backwards for the sake of his audience, but this suggestion will not bear weight. First, *Opticks* (1704) was clearly not intended for an audience unprepared to consider new evidence, at least, evidence such as Newton could conceive of it. Second, while the mathematical consequences of Newton's argument lead to perfectly good lens geometry, they also predict a prismatic refraction pattern exactly the reverse of that found in nature and which Newton could have checked easily by observation. Yet he stuck to his principles.

God is not alone the source of first principles. Political truths, economic laws, supposedly immutable systems of logic all may function as the general axioms Bacon warned against. Even science itself, past and accepted science of course, can be used rhetorically to justify a rejection of the reports others attribute to their senses, calculations, observations, and experiments. Arthur C. Clarke notes that a Leipzig newspaper of 1839 found that Daguerre's report of his invention of photography "affronted both German science and God, in that order":

> The wish to capture evanescent reflections is not only impossible, as has been shown by thorough German investigation, but . . . the will to do so is blasphemy. God created man in his own image, and no man-made machine may fix the image of God. . . . One can straightway call the Frenchman Daguerre, who boasts of such unheard-of things, the fool of fools.

One can also suggest that this is probably the writing of a journalist untrained in science and that we are far beyond his skepticism. This suggestion, too, would be wrong.

Lewis Thomas is an honored and important working scientist and the admired director of the Memorial Sloan-Kettering Cancer Center. He is also an elegant essayist. His primary work is biological, but he certainly has more right than the Leipzig journalist, or the average contemporary novelist, to offer a meditation on "Computers":

> Sooner or later, there will be real human hardware, great whirring, clicking cabinets intelligent enough to read magazines and vote, able to think rings around the rest of us. [But] Before we begin organizing sanctuaries and reservations for our software selves, lest we vanish like the whales, here is a thought to relax with.
>
> Even when technology succeeds in manufacturing a machine as big as Texas to do everything we recognize as human, it will still be, at best, a single individual. This amounts to nothing, practically speaking. To match what we can do, there would have to be 3 billion of them with more coming down the assembly line, and I doubt that anyone will put up the money, much less make room. . . . I think we're safe for a long time ahead.

"A long time ahead" needs to be judged from 1974, the publication date of *The Lives of a Cell,* Thomas's collection of essays that won a National Book Award. Before the 1970s had expired, the so-called "microchip revolution" made clear that Thomas's computer "as big as Texas" was a gross fiction accepted to justify "a thought to relax with." And why, by the way, should the ultimate computer be *only* as capable as a human being? Perhaps 3 of them will do what 3 billion of us have done. Thomas's arguments, after all, are based not on the relevant data, computer science, but on biology, the study of social systems, and wishful thinking. Man may like to think—and may act—as if he were the measure of all things, he may believe that moons invisible to the naked eye are for that very reason both useless and impossible, but again and again in the past four centuries science has labored to show us that this is not so.

The four arguments just quoted start from different first principles for reasons having something to do with the nearly unarguable developments of science. Newton may be able to deduce the nature of light from his ideas of God, but Thomas needs to deduce the nature of technology from his ideas of nature. What these four arguments have in common, however, in addition to the rhetorical structure of argument from first principles, is a fundamental conservatism. Each of these arguments, in its own way, tells us that things don't change. Science, of course, and particularly applied science, technology, Bacon's "effecting all things possible," does manifestly change things, things like life span, types of work, means of communication, size of societies, and so much more. Yet precisely because the world since Bacon has been so much changed, people feel often the need of "a thought to relax with." Change is danger, while arguments from first principles leave first principles unchanged. They leave us "safe for a long time ahead."

Bacon's alternative rhetoric based on the senses, observation, calculation, theorizing and experimentation leads from data to middle axioms and then to general principles. If done honestly, the end principles may not be those in wide vogue. Hence, the rhetoric of science, like science itself, involves risk of change. This rhetoric clearly undercuts the secure stasis toward which both individuals and society have frequently tended. Popular belief has it that scientists, unlike the majority of us, do not stick blindly by their first principles, but rather, follow Bacon's second path and build carefully and dispassionately from data to general axioms, even if those general axioms confound the truths they learned in their youths. While this may sometimes be true, it is certainly not always true. Einstein did as much as any person to throw out old principles in favor of new, yet he is famous for his lifelong rejection of the validity of quantum mechanics: "I refuse to believe that God plays dice with the universe." Max Planck, who won the Nobel Prize (1918) for propounding quantum mechanics, knew full well that mere data and reasoning would not convince his peers:

> A new scientific truth does not triumph by convincing its opponents and making them see the light, but rather because its opponents eventually die, and a new generation grows up that is familiar with it.

From the very beginning of modern science, the problem of persuasion has been at least as much a rhetorical one as an empirical one. David A. Kronick has studied the self-conscious activities of scientists aimed at increasing their own credibility. First, there was the formation of scientific societies. An established group obviously had more believability than a lone witness to some unheard-of phenomenon. Second, the societies published journals. I see this as crucial since the commission of one's words to print lends them the respectability of permanence, a uniquely desirable characteristic in an argument unconsciously being rejected because it supports change. Third, the process of peer review developed, so that scientists could give mutual support to their credibility by underscoring each other's integrity. Sense data and logic were not, finally, the heart of the issue. As Kronick notes, "Authority and credibility in science . . . derived ultimately from the author or originator of the work" and "the authority of the evidence is directly related to the reliability of the witness." If we are asked to accept an argument that the world must be reconceived, then at least we ought to be able to rely on the arguer being comfortably one of us, an exemplar of our culture, which we were led to expect was indeed the natural order of the world.

In the manner of Bacon's argument from the senses, I would like to offer an observation. When I took physics in college, my classmates and I were taught the elegance and meaning of Newton's Law of Universal Gravitation. Then, in the laboratory, two-person teams of us were given special apparatus by which we would ourselves be able to confirm this law and incidentally derive G, the Universal Gravitational Constant. This apparatus consisted of two small dumbbells made of lead, whose mass we could ascertain with a balance and whose separation we could determine by using a ruler. We then hung these carefully in midair by strings through their crossbars and with a stopwatch measured the time it took for the balls to approach each other. Of course, our reference book gave us the correct value for G and one team was quite delighted to find that their lab technique was good enough to get within 3% of that sacred figure. We all came away persuaded that the laboratory exercise had confirmed the theory of the lecture. Newton's first principle was secure.

But Newton's first principle should not have been secure. The implicit argument of that class was not from data but from first principles supplied by lecturer and text writer. The data tell us clearly that at best Newton's figure is within 3% of that achieved by the students. The credibility established by working in teams obviously did not insure reliability of results if reliability is measured by consistency. We can explain these problems—and we did—by using another first principle, the "experimental error." Experimental error was introduced by the infinitesimal differences in the balances and rulers and watches and in each team's abilities to read these. Arguing now as Bacon does, I propose that we should not have concluded that our activities confirmed the Law of Universal Gravitation, but rather, that they suggested the Law of Universal Experimental Error.

Most philosophies of science rely on the notion of replicability of results, objectivity of observation, and prediction. Each of these ideals, we are told, may be checked by the activities of independent researchers. And I surely do not want to assert that such checking never happens. However, Mendel's classic paper on genetics lay unheeded in a Bavarian library for thirty-five years; a full generation passed between the publication of Sir Cyril Burt's studies of the development of separated twins and the radical reinterpretation of those data; and some modern experiments, like the computer run that presumably confirms the four-color theorem, are so complex that they cannot be checked, much less confirmed, themselves. Working scientists, like students in a college laboratory, may do their best to check things out, but finally must rely for the vast bulk of their data on the probity and accuracy of equipment manufacturers, publishers of reference books, peers, and, most of all, teachers. John Ziman has focused on this wide network of trust and tried to use it to show that scientific knowledge is unique:

> Ideally the general body of scientific knowledge should consist of facts and principles that are firmly established and accepted without serious doubt, by an overwhelming majority of competent, well-informed scientists.

Ziman has defined, it seems to me, a *discourse community*. The criteria defining "competent" and "well-informed" are criteria of the scientists themselves. The body of knowledge is "factual" only as it is taken as factual by the discourse community. Membership in the discourse community comes from acceptance of the body of fact already held. In short, science is defined not so much by real world effect as by the sociology of authority. Voodoo and acupuncture may be reported efficacious again and again, but they are as scientifically impossible as the moons of Jupiter and electromagnetic wave phenomena and Daguerrotypes and small but capacious computers until they are "accepted" by the discourse community which won, in the seventeenth and eighteenth centuries, the guardianship of science.

The winning of this guardianship came hard, as we have seen. It required a conscious effort of scientists to establish their own credibility, the overwhelming of an impulse to stasis common to both society at large and the community of scientists, and, of course, the real and significant products of science. One could hardly dispute the reality of the profound and brilliant and wonderful and terrifying imaginings and creations of science. But the changes science wrought in habits of mind, as manifested in the use of the rhetoric of science, were not nearly so complete as the changes science wrought in the physical components of human life. Despite the supposed philosophic implications of science, the argument from first principles remains a fixed rhetorical habit today just as it did in the past. Whether the discourse community takes its first principles from science or from theology, the approach to the world revealed in rhetoric may go unchanged.

Those sensitive to change and those prepared to embrace a rhetoric of change need not be scientists. While scientists address a discourse community of scientists, novelists address a wider discourse community of the literate. If we can accept the earlier argument that science and poetry are not ontologically antagonistic, then we might well hope to find fictional uses of the rhetoric of science not only in Butler's description of the river valley but in texts scattered from Bacon's time to the present. These uses would change as the prevailing first principles of the time evolved under the impact of the advances wrought by science and as the consequent needs of artists also changed. Jeremy Warburg suggests that one index of an artist's most profound understanding of his world is the construction of his metaphors.

Herbert L. Sussman has taken up this useful notion and asserted that:

> Alone among the industrial novelists, indeed alone among English writers of prose fiction up to Wells and Kipling, Dickens's imagination had so absorbed machine technology that he could use it as vehicle rather than tenor. . . .

An example of the rhetoric that Sussman seems to have in mind occurs in the second chapter of *Hard Times* (1854):

> [Schoolmaster Gradgrind] seemed a kind of cannon loaded to the muzzle with facts, and prepared to blow [his pupils] clean out of the regions of childhood at one discharge. He seemed a galvanizing apparatus, too, charged with a grim mechanical substitute for the tender young imaginations that were to be stormed away.
> "Girl number twenty," said Mr. Gradgrind, squarely pointing with his square forefinger, "I don't know that girl. Who is that girl?"

In addition to the technological metaphors, this passage implies a critique of the rhetoric of science: mere enumeration is not the same as understanding. Gradgrind at first thinks he knows Sissy Jupe because he "has her number," but he is at bottom human enough to realize that he does not know her—yet. Gradgrind himself is described in terms of calculation and observation:

> Thomas Gradgrind, sir. A man of realities. A man of facts and calculations. A man who proceeds upon the principle that two and two are four, and nothing over, and who is not to be talked into allowing for anything over.

The very rhetoric of science is here used to adduce a damning datum about Gradgrind, that he follows the rhetoric of argument from first principles, albeit scientific first principles. Thus Dickens offers in a single chapter a critique of the rhetoric of science and of the rhetoric that science might change. Clearly this mid-nineteenth-century novel has not merely "absorbed machine technology" but has grappled with it in questioning the definition of humanity and the nature of progress. Alan J. Friedman has pointed out that science still serves to manifest extraordinary fictional complexity:

> Today we can see physics selected energetically as a tool for the purpose of making fiction. The most effective of these interactions of physics with fiction, in the works of Pynchon and Coover, have physics serving as a metaphor.

But this potentially complex metaphorical use of science and technology goes back at least, once again, to Francis Bacon. The inhabitants of New Atlantis reject the notion that a small evil may serve well to forestall a greater evil:

> . . . they say farther that there is little gained in this, for that the same vices and appetites do still remain and abound, unlawful lust being like a furnace, that if you stop the flames altogether, it will quench, but if you give it any vent, it will rage.

Such metaphors might be expected from the pen of the thinker so sensitive to the implications of change that he suggested the very rhetorical opposition that later writers would manipulate.

The historical progress of the rhetoric of science is primarily a record of the interplay of felt authority. In the early seventeenth century, when the prevailing first principles in the artist's discourse community were theological, Bacon, as we have seen, used the authority of theology to validate the rhetoric of science. As science and technology—and the persuasiveness of the rhetoric of science—changed the world and the way people viewed it, the competing authorities changed their balance until today the rhetoric of science is used to lend authority to religion, as in such spiritual works of science fiction as Olaf Stapledon's *Star Maker* (1937) or Arthur C. Clarke's *2001* (1968). This historical turnabout is sufficiently complicated, as the examples of Butler and Dickens should make clear, that it is worth tracing in some detail.

In *Other Worlds* (1657), Cyrano de Bergerac makes obvious his admiration for what to him was modern science. On the sun, Cyrano's Earthling narrator meets Campanella who is hurrying to a rendezvous with Descartes:

> When I asked him . . . in what esteem he held [Descartes's] *Physics*, he answered that it should be read with no less respect

than that [with] which the pronouncements of the oracles are heard. 'Not that the natural sciences have no need, like the other sciences, to be examined critically for axioms they do not prove;' he added, 'but the principles of *his* are so simple and so natural that once they are supposed, there is no other system which fits all the evidence better.'

Although Cyrano's admiration for science is clear, and although he uses the rhetoric of science in a rudimentary form by proposing observation and testing of theory against fact, he still finds it helpful to support the argument with a quasi-religious term like "oracle" and to defend the author of perhaps the most famous argument derived from first principles, the "Cogito ergo sum."

By the time of Defoe, the rules of evidence for Baconian science had come, at least for some discourse community, to stand for the rules of evidence for the real world. A standard definition of that science is:

... the observation, identification, description, experimental investigation, and theoretical explanation of natural phenomena.

Notice how in *Robinson Crusoe* (1719) Defoe unobtrusively adopts precisely this pattern of activities to lend authority to the narrative and to implicitly argue his protagonist's capacity to "effect all things possible." The following is Robinson's diary entry for April 22:

The next morning I began to consider of means to put this resolve [to build a shelter] in execution, but I was at a great loss about my tools [*observation*]; I had three large axes and abundance of hatchets (for we carried the hatchets for traffic with the Indians) [*identification*], but with much chopping and cutting knotty hardwood, they were full of notches and dull [*description*], and though I had a grindstone, I could not turn it and grind my tools too [*experimentation*]. This cost me as much thought [*theoretical explanation*] as a statesman would have bestowed upon a grand point of politics, or a judge upon the life and death of a man. At length I contrived a wheel with a string, to turn it with my foot, that I might have both my hands at liberty. I had never seen any such thing in England, or at least not to take notice how it was done, though since I have observed it is very common there;

besides that, my grindstone was very large and heavy. This machine cost me a full week's work to bring it to perfection.

Besides reproducing the steps of science given by the dictionary definition, this passage also incorporates a number of other traits commonly associated with science: quantification, testing of hypotheses, and independent replication by another investigator in a different locale. In this passage the rhetoric of science stands full blown and alone, accepted as the authoritative language by which to reflect the world. While the other examples of the rhetoric of science we have noted admix it with other rhetorics, this one does not. There are at least two possible causes for this wholehearted acceptance.

First, by this date in the eighteenth century, there existed a populous discourse community that accepted the rhetoric of science. Although this rhetoric does come in for occasional satire, as in the exaggerated geometric description of the means of navigation of the floating city of Laputa in the third book of Swift's *Gulliver's Travels* (1726), that satire is motivated by the ineffectuality of science, the failure of the claims of Bacon, rather than the later fear of technology on the rampage. Second, Robinson's change in his environment is not a change in the reader's environment but rather an establishment of Robinson's dominion over the island and a transformation of that island into a comfortable extension of then contemporary England. Thus, for a moment, the rhetoric of science holds sway.

A generation later, as we have seen, Voltaire used the authority of the rhetoric of science to attack what he saw as the superstitions of organized religion. In *Micromegas* (1752), the title character is a giant from Sirius who visits Earth and other planets and occasions much satirical comment. The one group to escape invidious comparison are the scientists:

> "Since you are of the small number of the wise," said he, "and in all likelihood do not engage in the trade of murder for hire, be so good as to tell me your occupation."
> "We anatomize flies," replied the philosopher, "we measure lines, we make calculations, we agree upon two or three points which we understand, and dispute upon two or three thousand that are beyond our comprehension."

While admiring this Socratic humility, Voltaire simultaneously uses the rhetoric of science to attack religion, as, for example, the unwarranted religious pride of "the gentleman inquisitors." The authority of the rhetoric of science having been established by Bacon, Cyrano, and a hundred thirty years of science, this rhetoric which began by borrowing authority from the Bible comes to be used to turn back the authority of the Church.

Once the rhetoric of science becomes a monolith in its own right, and once science begins to change the world in more frightening ways, the uses of the rhetoric of science in fiction become more complex. Probably every imaginable use of this rhetoric has been tried, but we can at least begin to understand the complexity of these developments by dividing the uses into four camps: those uses intended to explore science both to favor it and to criticize it, and those uses that borrow the authority of science to warrant discussion of other matters than science, both in fabulous fiction and in normative fiction. We can briefly discuss these in order.

Darko Suvin has cogently called *Robinson Crusoe* "Verne's great model." Just as Defoe favored science enthusiastically, so did Verne. At the conclusion of *Twenty Thousand Leagues Under the Sea* (1869), Verne's narrator, Professor Aronnax, has one final reflection on the complex character of Captain Nemo, his erstwhile captor: "May the judge disappear and the scientist continue his peaceful exploration of the seas!" Typical of Verne's attitude is the delight Conseil, the Professor's attendant, has in discovering "A left-handed shell!" in Nemo's collection.

The famous long naturalistic catalogues and passages of taxonomic detail do much to give this novel its tone, a tone comically varied by the satire directed against Aronnax's arrogance of knowledge through Conseil's unquestioning acceptance and Ned Land's practical incredulity. When Aronnax wants to teach the Canadian harpooner the fine points of ichthyology and asks Land if he knows how fish are classified, the man of the sea replies simply and sensibly that "They're classified into those you can eat and those you can't." At first, this reply, which seems to give the professor his comeuppance, may seem to thwart the rhetoric of science. But a closer examination reveals, rather, that Ned has properly used his sense experience to make an important experimental distinction. The satire is not of science but of impracticality based on a lofty removal from the world, the same criticism Swift offered while leaving science intact. Fundamentally, Verne, like DeFoe, fosters science by adopting its rhetoric regardless of what he says in that rhetoric. This Vernean enthusiasm can even effect a rapprochement between science and art. As Arthur Conan Doyle has the secretary of his fictional scientific society conclude after examining all the evidence retrieved from *The Lost World* (1912):

> Apparently the age of romance was not dead, and there was common ground upon which the wildest imaginings of the novelist could meet the actual scientific investigations of the searcher for truth.

This more or less pure enthusiasm comes down to the present in the rhetoric of Isaac Asimov and Larry Niven and a host of others.

Wider critical importance has been given to works exploring science and criticizing it. Gradgrind's girl number twenty becomes the numbered characters of Eugene Zamiatin's *We* (1920), Ayn Rand's *Anthem* (1938), and George Lucas's *THX1138* (1971). Zamiatin carries the rhetoric of science to an exaggerated extreme when his narrator, D-503, notes in record 24 that "$L = F(D)$, love is the function of death." The possibility for this exaggeration derives not from the fact of science in our lives, however, but from our literate acquaintance with the rhetoric of science. In a world such as ours, even the critique of science must speak the language of science, and so it often does.

The language of science lends its authority to fictions focused on nonscientific matters. H. G. Wells's early fabulations of social criticism, such as *The Time Machine* (1895) and *The War of the Worlds* (1898), fixed the pattern for a powerful type of social and psychological exploration carried down to the present with works like William Golding's *Lord of the Flies* (1954) and Anthony Burgess's *A Clockwork Orange* (1962). Wells's Time Traveller spends his whole first chapter arguing for the possibility of time travel and then demonstrating his working model; the anti-colonial story of Martian invasion begins with observation of the flares on Mars, the construction of hypotheses about them, and

final refutation. In parallel ways, Golding motivates his anthro-
pological tale by the prospect of nuclear war and Burgess justifies
his exaggeration of behaviorist theory by displacement to the
future.

In more normative works, the rhetoric of science flourished
not only in Verne's pages but in Zola's, with minute observation
of social conditions and construction of model social situations
for testing ideas about psychodynamics. Zola's rhetoric is with
us yet, amalgamated into the tradition that we have come to take
as normative, realism. But that term is so variable that we must
recognize that the rhetoric of science has become a potential tool
in the arsenal of every modern writer.

Most fiction seems to cater to the values of its audience, to
entertain and to remind. If fiction shakes us up, it usually does
so by an appeal to some suppressed or forgotten or underused
value, rather than to some new value. In this sense, fiction is
predominantly reflection and conservative, and one would expect it to favor, as it once did, argument from first principles. Yet
we have seen that the much riskier rhetoric of science, while
serving many masters for many purposes over many years, has
come to dominate fiction as a source of authority. This development is certainly, in part, a result of the success science has
had in supplanting other sources of authority outside the realms
of fiction, but why should fiction respond to these developments?
Quite simply, fiction has as strong a need to persuade as does
scientific discourse. In part this conclusion follows from our earlier discussions of the nature of scientific and other knowledge
and of the effects of rhetoric on discourse communities. In part,
however, it follows from a matter peculiar to fiction. The classic
fictional treatment of the fear of science is Mary Shelley's *Fran-
kenstein* (1818). Yet even this book begins with a Preface as-
serting that:

> The event on which this fiction is founded has been supposed,
> by Dr. [Erasmus] Darwin, and some of the physiological writers
> of Germany, as not of impossible occurrence.

Shelley had written a palpable fable and she knew that its full
effect depended on authorizing some possibility of belief.

The rhetoric of science in fiction is not merely a modern overlay on storytelling, nor is it employed, except fortuitously, to convey newly discovered information about the world. Once upon a time fiction—which obviously is not true—took its authority from the Muse; at other times from the Bible. Neither of these sources of authority would do for Shelley, but authority has always to be found somewhere if we are to distinguish the lies that tell truths from just plain lies. Today, whether we are conscious of it or not, our rules of evidence are encoded in the rhetoric of science. In the fiction we call novels and in unadmitted fiction too, when we think we are testing to discover whether the assertions we read are true, we are really listening for the voice of the Muse.

4

Cy Chauvin

IAN WATSON'S MIRACLE MEN

Ian Watson follows a tradition in science fiction that emphasizes the genre's nonliterary values. He believes that science fiction has more importance as an "evolutionary tool," as a means to alter our consciousness, than as literature. His novels and short stories constantly question the credibility of our present view of reality; he is obsessed with epistemological problems. Nearly all science fiction inherently questions the nature of reality, but this matter is more than implied in Watson's work; it is a central theme. Watson also believes that science fiction will eventually "wither away" as it fulfills its evolutionary role—and so will the novel, for the human condition is not a fixed matter, unchanging down through the ages. Despite—or perhaps because of—these heretical views, he is one of the most important new writers of SF.

The nonliterary values of science fiction have often been debated, but little defined, since form and content are so closely linked in literature. Science fiction writers have always wanted to change the world—hence the great tradition of antiutopian novels. And does anyone imagine, as Gregory Benford pointed out, that science fiction is now taught in the classroom for its literary excellence? Thus when Watson writes, "Quite a lot of SF today is taking refuge in literature," science fiction writers know what he means, and it isn't that he's for poorly written fiction. Instead:

> The point is that the human condition isn't enduring; nor is it art; nor is Man as we know him/her. . . . We are an evolving, changing species. Literature is part of the evolutionary process. It has meaning only within this biological and social context. And what is unique about SF is that it consciously takes as its subject matter this sense of Man changing within and by contact with the physical universe at large . . . most Great Literature assumes that the human condition is unchanging down through the ages.

Watson's first published novel is *The Embedding* (1973). "To embed" means "to set in among another mass; to fix in the mind, memory." Watson's novel uses the word in both meanings, both environmental and mental (linguistic). "The basic plan of language reflects our biological awareness of the world that has evolved us."

The novels tells three interconnected stories. One concerns Chris Sole, a linguist who works in an experimental hospital in England. Three groups of children are kept in special environments, isolated from all contact with the normal world, and taught specially designed languages. One group is in a Logic World, another in an Alien World, and a third (Sole's group) in an Embedded World. The third group is taught a special "self-embedded" language. Language processing depends upon the volume of information that the brain can store short-term. In order to understand this sentence, for instance, one must be able to connect the meanings of the first word in the sentence through the last, embedding each until one finishes reading the sentence. Each sentence we read or hear is a fresh creation, unlike the signals animals use, which are fixed and unvarying. Each sentence is new because of the recursive feature of language—we have rules for doing the same thing more than once in a sentence. (Watson gives this example: "The dog *and* the cat *and* the bear ate.") This is a self-embedding process, one that the children in Chris Sole's special environment are taught, only to an extreme degree, in an attempt to achieve a totality of meaning—to connect *all* the information they know, together, at once. The children are also given a drug (PSF) to help speed up their learning functions.

There are some moral questions raised by these experiments and especially the children's isolation. Sole is upset by these questions; indeed, he seems to love his experimental group more than his own son (he calls them "my children"). One of the other scientists, Ms. Summers, tells him to think of "all the children that are going to be born before today's over—or wiped out by accident tonight! Do you think it matters one scrap that a dozen ... are brought up ... in somewhat unusual circumstances?" The children, incidentally, are war-orphans. When a visitor asks if the children's brains have been altered surgically for the experiment, Sole explodes in anger. "Christ no! ... That's a bloody immoral suggestion."

In Brazil, Pierre Darriand (a French anthropologist and friend of Sole's) has discovered an unique South American tribe, the Xemahoa. The tribe has two languages, one for everyday use, and one (Xemahoa B) for special religious ceremonies that is spoken under the influence of a fungi drug. This latter language has some relation to the artificial language Sole is studying with his experimental subjects in England. Darriand also believes that if he can learn Xemahoa B he might also understand *Nouvelles Impressions d'Afrique* by Raymond Roussel, a self-embedded poem that he has been trying to understand for years. An American-Brazilian dam project threatens to engulf the Indians' homeland, however, and destroy both their way of life and the special fungi they use in their rituals.

These two separate plot threads come together when contact is made with the Sp'thra, aliens from outer space, who offer the secrets of interstellar space travel for "the widest possible knowledge of language." Chris Sole is among the special delegation that makes contact with the aliens. The aliens' quest is in part mystical. "You might say we trade in realities," says Ph'theri, their spokesperson. The aliens are building a "language moon," and compiling the "reality programme" of all languages. They are driven to their quest by "the Bereft Love we feel for the Change Speakers." The Change Speakers have passed beyond this reality. "The universe here embeds us in it. But not them." The aliens hope to follow the Change Speakers in some way, once having completed their task:

> The Change Speakers desired something when they phased with
> the Sp'thra—what it was we did not understand. They themselves
> were hurting with love. Our signal trading quest is to cancel the
> great sense of sadness, so that we Sp'thra can be left alone again—
> without that vibration in our minds, imprinted so many centuries
> ago by their passage. . . . We are haunted by the Change Speakers,
> by this ghost of love, which is pain.

The Sp'thra and Sole negotiate. In return for the information on
space travel, the aliens want "six language units" from as widely
scattered areas as possible—a euphemism, it turns out, for an
adult human brain. Just before he meets with the aliens, Sole
happens to receive a letter from Darriand describing the Indian
tribe and the self-embedded language. The Sp'thra become en-
thusiastic when they are told of the discovery; they see the possibility of ending their quest here.

The Sp'thra's belief that the widest possible knowledge of
language might lead to an understanding of the reality program
of all languages and thus an understanding of the underlying
structure of reality itself is not merely a whimsical science fiction
concept, thrown in to add verisimilitude to another novel. It is
a true possibility. Watson has pointed out elsewhere that all
human beings, "possess a common market in meaning based on
the biological systems of emotional and purposive behaviour
they all share." If the environmental constraints that shape life
also shape intellectual structures in the same way, then we can
hope for a structural similarity in alien languages. He does caution us, however, that:

> . . . if the structure of reality is indeed mirrored in language, this
> in fact *prevents* language from articulating the structure of reality.
> In which case, to quote the logician Quine, "we do better simply
> to say the sentence and so not speak about language but about the
> world." One can either speak about language, or about the world;
> but not about both at once, using language. The purpose of lan-
> guage *is* language; there is no underlying significance. Thus it
> would be pointless to hunt for some universal significance which
> underlies, and links, the set of possible alien languages. It would
> be inarticulable; opaque; ungraspable.

Watson's next novel, *The Jonah Kit* (1975), combines whales and the discovery of a new cosmology, "The Footsteps of God." Paul Hammond discovers and promotes this new cosmology as its prophet. Hammond finds discrepancies in the microwave background radiation caused by the initial creation of the universe from one solid "Egg" form, and theorizes that we live in a shadow universe left behind after the real universe was formed. His reasoning is that the expansion of the original Egg occurred at a rate of two light years per second! At that speed each particle would reach infinite mass and have an infinitely strong gravitational field, and thus collapse in on itself, like a miniature black hole. "The fabric of space can't grow fast enough to contain such an explosion," says Hammond, ". . . so it must have been inwards."

Hammond's theory raises many protests, some concerning its substance, others concerning its presentation (for if nothing else, Hammond is a showman and promoter). The most interesting objection is raised by an Italian journalist, Gianfranco Morrelli:

> You are in effect denying authenticity to the universe, correct? Yet doesn't modern Physics say that the observer plays a role in creating the reality he observes? That he is by no means neutral? . . . The paradox that we—the human race, as a consensus of observers—are every moment engaged in choosing the type of universe we inhabit. We must choose, and what we choose will come into being, *so*!

Watson explicates this theory in his article, "Toward An Alien Linguistics":

> . . . a Universe is quite literally *meaningless* in the absence of any awareness of that Universe. But awareness requires life—which requires the presence of elements heavier than hydrogen. These can be produced by thermonuclear cookery inside suns over a time span of several billion years. This length of time is only available in a universe the size of ours. . . . So Dicke . . . arrives at the idea of a "biological selection of physical constraints." There appears to be a numerical relationship between the total estimated number of particles in the universe, the radius of the universe at its maximum point of expansion, the size of an elementary particle, the ratio between electrical and gravitational forces, and several

other so-called "big numbers." This relationship indicates a universe where [all these factors] are linked to one another structurally—such that a per cent difference either way in one of the constants would produce an uninhabitable cosmos. Why are these values as they are, in the first place? How are they chosen? They cannot be influenced or determined by any previous cycle of the universe—if we accept, as seems probable, that our universe will ultimately collapse into a Black Hole and undergo probabilistic scattering so that no laws or constants are preserved. Rather, according to John Wheeler's remarkable suggestion, we must admit that in some way the universe is brought into being by the participation of those who participate in it.

While Hammond is involved in spreading his new cosmology, the Russians have been experimenting with mind transfer. A six-year-old boy who defects to the West seems to have the mind of a dead cosmonaut (imperfectly) imprinted upon him. A blind poet and musician dying of cancer has had his mind translated into a computer abstract and imprinted upon that of a sperm whale, code name "Jonah." Jonah communicates via radio with a computer complex on Sakhalin, and the Russian scientists discover that groups of sperm whales, nosing together in a star formation near the surface of the ocean (often observed by sailors), form a "Thought Complex," a biological computer of tremendous power. From the viewpoint of Jonah, these groups seem to have mystical importance. For political reasons, the Russians are asked to send Hammond's theory to Jonah while he is participating in one of the Thought Complexes, to confirm or deny it.

The whales' conclusion is a signal of distress "modified by something else" sent to all kachalots (toothed whales). Within an hour, whales, porpoises, and even narwhales ("with the long twisted unicorn horn") swim to the shore and throw themselves up on the beaches to die. They reject Hammond's theory. But what is happening, according to Morrelli, is a split between our universe and that of the whales'—they do not believe in Hammond's cosmology, while "it's almost as though we have no choice—can't observe anything else," says Richard, one of Hammond's unhappy colleagues. One Japanese scientist views the whales' suicide as a matter of honor, a *seppuku*: "Would you accept the invasion of alien beings of your soul?" Morrelli explains that the whales have "subtracted" themselves from our universe, and chosen a positive one. Reality has branched. "Yet we still live in a rational world, it seems, so we have to rationalize their disappearance. They have seemed to die. . . . Truth is, they have escaped." He suggests that in their world all of humanity may have seemed to rush to the ocean, and drown itself.

The influence of Watson's three years as a lecturer in Tokyo surfaces most clearly in this novel—indeed, Watson wrote in *Vector* that, "Japan was the big mental earthquake. . . . I started writing SF as a survival strategy." Nigel Sellars has interpreted all of Watson's novels in terms of two Japanese concepts: *mono no aware* (literally, "the pathos of things") and *hoganbiki* (or sympathy with the loser). But *The Jonah Kit* is among Watson's least satisfying novels because of the distancing of the characters. The fragmentation of character viewpoints, perhaps vital for informational purposes, vastly lessens the intensity of the novel. We do not know any character well, although we know each one's opinions and theories on the current situation. The Russian scientist Katya is the most sympathetic character because she suffers a tragedy. Her lover was the dying poet, now the whale, and his translation has left a mindless body, the cancer temporarily stopped by the shock of the mind's transfer.

The Martian Inca (1977) is a better novel, perhaps technically Watson's best. It opens with the crash landing of a returning Russian space probe filled with dirt from Mars. It crashes in Bolivia and infects thirty-two people in a small village with a mysterious disease. The only ones who survive are two who have not been treated by doctors, Julio Capac, an ambitious young Indian, and Angelina Sonco, his lover. Both have undergone a transformation in the structure of their minds. Julio sees clearly for the first time the contradictions of the "uneasy coexistence of Workers' Unions, People's Government, Army, Church . . . together with an Indian past." He declares himself an Inca, and leads a revolution to restore the Incan ways:

> They [the Indians] were all asleep. Yet they still had their language, which the Incas had called *Runa Simi*, Speech of Man—because it was so strong, so flexible, so fine. Why, the early priests

had been scared to catechize their Indian flocks in it—and their God-sayings in Spanish and Latin were the ignorant mumblings of barbarian conquerors beside it. With that tool alone, the Incas hadn't needed wheels or horses, jeeps or aircraft to make the Andes human.

Angelina's metamorphosis is more personal. She realizes how much of her life has been affected by a dead friend, Justina, who was murdered. The experience "fouls" men for her, and she suppresses the memory of Justina's death. "All I really saw was what was wrong with me before and how it should never be again. Justina had been writing my life, and I didn't know it. I found how to rewrite." The Martian disease clears her mind rather than obsessing it with a vision of power. Her thoughts are clarified, but she realizes her ignorance, unlike Julio, who believes he has all the answers. She warns Julio against undertaking his conquest before knowing their own transformed minds.

Interwoven with this story is one centering on three American astronauts speeding towards Mars. They are to set up a solar reflector in orbit called *Warming Pan*, which will heat the carbon dioxide frozen in the Martian polar ice caps, causing it to evaporate and, they hope, bring about a greenhouse effect and warm the entire planet. This process, called terraforming, would make Mars inhabitable and is the major reason the space voyage has been granted funding.

The astronauts are obviously interested in the unusual Martian disease and its effects. As a precaution, only two of the astronauts are sent down to the surface of the planet, while the other remains in orbit with *Warming Pan*. Silverman, one of the two who venture out, cuts the foot of his suit while digging in the Martian soil and contracts the disease. His later conversation with Oates, his companion, reveals that he understands what has happened to him much more clearly than Julio.

Mutations aren't just random. They can't be because mutations move towards ... generic niches—geometrical niches, niches of structure, as surely as birds and beasts fill up all possible ecological niches.... [Mutations] get pushed down, till the [gene] pool's saturated. Till the time is ripe. *Then* they erupt. In a Big Change. I'm talking about the Big Leaps, not about modifying the shape of a toenail or eyelash. The change from No Language to Language. . . . A change of that order.

In "Towards An Alien Linguistics," Watson wrote:

How does living matter describe itself, in order to perpetuate itself? Are genetic instructions simply ordinary molecules? No, they are more. They are ordinary molecules endowed with *symbolic properties*. It is not the structure of molecules as such, but the internal self-interpretation of their structure as *symbols* that is the basis of life.

Silverman believes that this "*seeing*," as he calls it, is the next evolutionary step for man, and on the order of Language. But it can only happen after humans have been born and grow up, for they must have some memories to "see" in this new way. One must be born first before one can be reborn. Of course, the exact nature of this transformation is difficult for both Silverman and Watson to convey—Oates thinks Silverman a little loony in his enthusiasm and nonstop conversation, and Watson can hardly express something outside our own experience, even if we suspect that he is the first up that new rung on the evolutionary ladder! Like Wally Oates, this glimmering of another consciousness is something we wouldn't understand unless we underwent it ourselves, and so we doubt the other's sanity (i.e., their view of the world). It hardly comes as a surprise, then, that Silverman infects Oates with the Martian disease.

Other writers of science fiction have linked madness with a new form of consciousness, notably Doris Lessing (in *Briefing for a Descent into Hell*, 1971) and Philip K. Dick. David Wingrove notes that Dick shares with Watson a fascination with the relationship between each individual's unique, private world and our shared reality. Dick's novels generally center around the breakdown of one character's private world, while Watson questions the agreed-upon assumptions that underpin our shared world. In an essay, he writes, "We are in the sort of universe we are in *because* we are here to observe it; what, then, is the connection between thought and reality, cosmologically?" Watson does try to explain this new sense of consciousness evolving through the character of Silverman: ". . . out of one model—of the world around me, in my brain—is being generalized a secondary model of the topology relationships permeating the first model: using memory as 'virtual' building blocks. . . . You can *remember* and see the real world at the same time. . . . it's the memory illusions—" Silverman says the phenomenon has happened under open brain surgery, as a strange aberration.

Miracle Visitors (1978) is Watson's most important and outrageous novel to date. It is important because it attempts, in its own terms, to establish new paradigms. Paradigms, as Thomas S. Kuhn wrote in *The Structure of Scientific Revolutions*, are, "universally recognised scientific achievements that, for a time, provide model problems and solutions to a community of practitioners." *Miracle Visitors*—even more strongly than Watson's other novels—challenges the nature of our established scientific beliefs. As James Blish has pointed out, "the most important scientific content in modern science fiction is the impossibilities." And Watson's suggested alternatives are argued so well that his impossibilities seem nearly possible, and our belief systems are irrevocably altered.

The novel is constructed in a manner similar to Watson's others—each character represents different viewpoints or interpretations of the main events of the novel. Michael Peacocke is a young man who is hypnotized by John Deacon for an experimental program. Under hypnosis, Michael reveals a UFO encounter. Deacon is surprised but curious, especially when his tape of the experience is mysteriously erased. He wants to examine Michael for his university Consciousness Research Group. Michael and his girlfriend Suzi are burned by a UFO encounter a short while later and discuss their experiences with Barry Shriver, an American ex-Air Force pilot who has had his own UFO experiences. In a close succession of events, the three men receive a phone call (while the phone is disconnected) warning them not to "ask—questions—about—flying—saucer—beings" and see a pterodactyl fly by their office. Michael is helped by Men in Black, Deacon's dog is decapitated, and Suzi meets a mysterious green swamp man. Deacon, grasping for explanations, suggests that there is a similarity between these UFO events and the Tibertan *tulpas*, which are "Living creatures created by a prolonged act of thought. . . . they're supposed to be actual tangible things . . . able to function independently in the real world." He suggests that the UFO events are of the same nature as the appearances of devils and angels in an earlier age.

While pedaling on his bicycle past the spot where he had his very first UFO encounter (which he did not consciously remember, until revealed by hypnotism by Deacon), Michael meets a strange tortoise-elephant alien, driving a Ford Thunderbird with Wyoming plates. "A voice hooted, 'It is safe. It is not one of them. It is something else. Please come! Safe. Please believe . . .'" Michael reluctantly climbs in, and they fly to the other side of the moon in the altered Ford auto!

The aliens are called the Gebraudi, and have been sent on a mission from Eta Cassiopeia. Michael is told that all humanity is part of the Unidentified; the UFO events are projections of the Whole Planetary Life system of Earth. Just as our bodies are made up of individual cells, which in turn support our conscious and subconscious mind, so the earthmind, the consciousness of earth, is made up of all the living creatures of Earth, animals and plants as well as humanity. The Gebraudi say the earth is sick; humanity has killed thousands of plants and animals which supported the earthmind, and replaced them with more human beings, buildings and machines. "You cannot grasp the Whole Planet Life system when you are merely the thought cells in it. Yet you can certainly upset its balance, and very sanity, by your collective attitude."

The Gebraudi mission is to cure the earthmind. They are in contact with the Unidentified of their own planet, and their own technology is very bio-organic, with adapted plants fulfilling the function of much machinery. They want Michael to join the group of humans already there and help place delicate bio-sensors at crucial acupunctures on earth, foci for activity of the Unidentified on earth, such as Glastonbury Tor, Dragon Hill by Uffington, Stonehenge, Silbury Hill. One of the women in the group tells Michael, "We couldn't tolerate it if the aliens came. We're too self-centered. We've infected the world. We've malformed it. . . . That's why it [the Unidentified] wiped out the first [Gebraudi] expedition." Deacon, meanwhile, has also taken a journey. He wakes up, mysteriously, in Cairo, Egypt, without a passport and no knowledge of how he has arrived there. He contacts Sheik Muradi, a Sufi, and author of *Consciousness: Ancient and Modern*. Muradi has been expecting him. He has been forewarned of Deacon's journey by Khidr, the Green Man, a Sufi saint, a secret guide who "often brought help beyond comprehension . . . he appeared at moments of insight and breakthrough." Khidr has given Muradi a book for Deacon, a worn brown volume of French magic. One of the diagrams in it matches that of one Michael drew under hypnosis, the supposed schematic for a gravity-propelled spaceship. More importantly, the Sufi seem better equipped intellectually than Deacon for dealing with the UFO events. Muradi says "Our way . . . seeks to evolve Man. It establishes communication with an ultimate source of knowledge. But this source can't be known directly. . . . Can you imagine a mind observing *all of itself*? If it were all busy observing, what would it be observing? Paradox!" Paradox does not disturb the Sufi; nor does new knowledge. "Real knowledge . . . forces people to develop new organs of perception; . . . thus evolution is made possible." Muradi also explains that in Deacon's jargon, "new organs of perception" means new states of consciousness.

It is discovered that Deacon took out enough money from the bank to cover the air fare from England to Egypt, but he still has no conscious awareness of his actions and insists to the press that he flew to Cairo in a state of "UFO-consciousness"! Deacon has a controversial meeting with the Consciousness Research Group, which wishes to drop funding for his activities. He tells them:

> The Phenomenon has always been with us in one form or another because it really relates to what you might call, information-wise, the "knowability" of the cosmos. It's a kind of evolutionary learning program which exists because of the way the universe is. It teaches by means of what is *unknown*. How else? It uses the medium of what is, at each and every stage, unknowable.

A short while after Michael returns to earth, he decides he must show Deacon and Shriver his amazing car, and, more importantly, have them meet the Gebraudi on the far side of the moon. Upon arrival, they find the Gebraudi base destroyed, seemingly crushed under tremendous pressure. A huge black *thing* (they can see no details, only its outline against the stars) descends in an attempt to crush them as well. The alternative theories that Watson is so fond of are suggested here by Deacon, who views their moon trip as a sort of *tulpa*—"Why not a phantom journey which had its own equal force of reality, one where driver and passengers could all be crushed to death against lunar lava or burst open in the emptiness of space at the very same time as the car impacted with a juggernaut lorry somewhere in England . . . ?"

They flee back to earth and crash land in the Colorado desert when the Thunderbird runs out of nuclear reaction mass. The apparition is still in pursuit of them, so they separate and run into the desert. Each reacts differently after this. Michael finally denies all that happened and Shriver is still trying to find hard proof for the authorities, while Deacon is transformed.

Deacon meets the black void in the desert and is absorbed by it. He finds it is consciousness without content, a mind, in Muradi's words, observing all of itself. Then the void becomes a vortex and firms into a craft, a UFO. And with him in the craft is Khidr, the Green Man, his body composed entirely of vegetables. This meeting is revelatory: every question Deacon asks Khidr is its own answer. "The universe, he realized, was an immense *simulation*: of itself, by itself . . . a progressive observation of itself from ever higher points of view. Each higher order was inaccessible to a lower order, yet each lower order was drawn towards the higher—teased by the suction of the higher. . . . The ultimate knowledge of the universe would *be* the universe itself; then subject and object would be one." The Gebraudi and the UFO events are all intrusions of this higher order into a lower-order world. They are miracles. Deacon then goes on an amazing journey—for once in the novel, a chapter is carried along almost without dialog—and appears at most of the climactic UFO events earlier in the novel, causing them! Then, after learning what he needs, he appears back on the desert and meets his rescuers. Like Silverman in *The Martian Inca*, he babbles and has only a partial ability to convey his transformation. But his insight is more accessible to the reader than Silverman's:

> When you investigate something, you change the nature of what
> you investigate. Impossible to intervene without altering reality.
> Physicists knew that well enough; they called it Indeterminacy.
> It was proof of the living texture of events and the ability of those
> who saw this to become—within their limits—conscious thinkers
> of reality.

Later:

> There are no casual proofs, only demonstrations. . . . You can never
> validate a system completely within the terms of that system. . . .
> Systems are only "proved"—they're only fully determined—by
> higher systems. . . . The force that evolves higher [systems] out
> of lower is nothing less than [the] basic separation of observer
> from observed, of consciousness from what it's conscious of. It's
> this inaccessibility—the pull of it!

And:

> How did one define an "entity"? Was it a single body cell, or the
> whole body? Or was it the whole ecology this body was part of?
> Where did one draw the line? Was a stone a separate object—or
> the single atoms that made it up? Or the much larger rock it must
> have fractured from? Or the whole desert environment? . . . a
> human being drew the line at such and such a point, yet actually
> it was quite arbitrary. Really, all the "separate" entities and objects
> in the world were more like amplitude peaks along a continuous
> line of being.

Deacon's whole philosophy of life has been altered; he feels
he is more in control of himself. At first he had desired research
grants and fame, and now he has surrendered himself to the force
that took him in the desert. After his return to England, his ideas
and actions are too outrageous for either his wife or his university
to accept, and Deacon himself desires a major change. Thus
when he meets a stranger who knows his name and offers him
a map of an alien city, a "one-way membrane, leading to another
state," he accepts eagerly. At this point, Watson achieves what

comes so rarely in his novels, a poetic intensity:

> The map stretched vastly now, becoming in reality what it had
> hitherto been the emblem of. As it became fully real to him, he
> stepped inside it with the stranger. . . .

The map of the city becomes the city. This makes perfect aesthetic sense, only it is not a metaphor, but an event that can be described only metaphorically, because it is not of our world.

John Deacon never returns; he becomes a missing person. "You are an enigma now," the stranger tells him, "you offer no proof, you can only offer clues." He can only return to the world miraculously now, a UFO event himself, as another Khidr, a secret guide.

Miracle Visitors, in the words of Brian Stableford, "suggests the possibility of modes of thought, forms of life and ways of understanding that presently wait outside the prison of our ideas"—more so even than Watson's earlier novels. It acts in a similar manner on the reader as the UFO events do upon the characters within the novel; Watson believes all science fiction should do this. The important matter is not the transformation of John Deacon, but of the reader. The characters in Watson's novels are only mouthpieces.

Yet Watson's novels would have more power if this were not the case; in part, his pantheon of characters weaken his works. As James Blish remarked about Frank Herbert, "as he tells an already complicated story, he complicates it further by jumping from one point of view to another." But it is more than that. Watson has great difficulty making his readers care about his characters; all his concern is with his theme. The characters have little depth and individuality, few differences that are of much consequence in the novel, and are as obsessed with unraveling the secrets of the universe as Watson. The human relationships are of less importance because the dramatic tension in the novels is focused elsewhere. Can an author write two stories of equal importance at once, a novel of emotions and a novel of scientific discovery? Or will there always be that dichotomy in science fiction? Except for perhaps his first novel, *The Embedding*, Watson hasn't tried. The viewpoint of his novels are split among so many characters as to dilute the importance of all. If his scientific concerns were handled in a similar fashion, his novels would be of no importance.

The most marvelous quality of Watson's work is his ability to brainwash his readers of their previous views of reality. He creates amazing theoretical assemblages, piling up detail upon detail, like the composer of an informational symphony, and one is left convinced. It is difficult for him to show in a dramatic way these theoretical creations, so instead the characters lecture one another, explaining them in great detail. This is awkward, and more of an old-fashioned than modern technique in science fiction, but in Watson's case it seems unavoidable.

Truly, Watson is writing in the shadow of *2001* and *Childhood's End*, and the ultimate themes of these works are his as well, but the sciences that interest him most are linguistics, theories of consciousness, biological evolution, and other areas rarely examined in SF. His work indicates a way to integrate the many forces that dominate our technologically oriented lives. He shows that the artist's and scientist's intensity are one, and in his public statements in essays and speeches, Watson has argued that science fiction should not be in a separate compartment in our lives (like too much of art) but should shape and change it. However, unlike John Deacon's stranger, he can offer us no map to transform our lives, only clues. "You offer no proof, you can only offer clues."

5

Donald M. Hassler

SCIENCE AT THE CROSSROADS IN HAL CLEMENT'S *THE NITROGEN FIX*

Mankind has always asked questions about questions. We want to understand *how* we know things, and we want to find out whether we will someday be able to know everything. The great myths about Prometheus and about the serpent in the Garden of Eden tell us that there are limits to our abilities to know, and most religions include beliefs about pride as opposed to humility. Modern science is based on the process of accumulating bits of knowledge about questions long before any larger answers to the questions can be known. In fact, the testing of scientific hypotheses by means of experiment assumes that some of the bits of information will be wrong.

A major category of science fiction, sometimes labeled "hard science fiction," is very much concerned with how science operates. Hal Clement, one of the most important writers of hard science fiction, has written many novels and short stories about the scientific method, among them *The Nitrogen Fix*, published in 1980. It is not only a good novel but also an interesting and important source of ideas about how we know things. A hard science fiction writer may often explore a line of reasoning for a long time through the telling of a number of stories, because such writers are particularly interested in ideas and they know that ideas, like organic chain molecules, can be added to continually.

Hal Clement's writing resembles the nature of scientific knowledge accumulated by scientists who cooperate in order to piece together larger theories out of smaller research results. He expands on his own earlier ideas and modifies them; like the scientist, he acknowledges that sometimes mistakes can lead to more knowledge. Naturally, all writers enlarge upon themes and images, but hard science fiction writers do this based on scientific thought, especially Clement, who likes to discuss ideas about ideas.

Clement has said that he first thought of the story for *The Nitrogen Fix* in 1958 in a talk he gave at Stone Hill College in New York. He outlined for those college students the possibility of an environmental and ecological disaster in the earth's atmosphere. He then worked carefully for two decades, weighing all the implications of that disaster he had imagined, attributing it to a plausible scientific mistake in biological engineering. Clement has said that the favorite part of a science fiction creation for him is the slide rule work, and he often takes a long time planning the details in the environment for a story. For example, as part of the work on his most famous novel, *Mission of Gravity* (1954), he wrote a nonfiction essay that describes the unusual physical characteristics of the planet Mesklin in that novel. This essay, complete with calculations and illustrations that he sketched to visualize the planetary system, is now printed as an "Afterword" to most editions of the novel. Although he has not yet published a nonfiction essay about the peculiar state of earth's environment in *The Nitrogen Fix*, he thought carefully about the details for a long time. During this time, he also wrote a number of short stories, novelettes, and another novel [*Ocean on Top* (1973)] about the energy crisis on earth and in the life cycle of other planets, as well as about the products of biological engineering. One novelette published in 1966, "The Mechanic," even features genetically engineered pseudolife sea creatures called zeowhales that appear again later in the plot of *The Nitrogen Fix*. Thus, Clement's manner of working out the extrapolation for this important novel was a combination of careful thinking and accumulating bits of knowledge that were tried out in other pieces of fiction over a fairly long period of time. As we shall see in the novel, he does not seem to believe in the immediate revelation of final knowledge or in final answers.

The opening scene of *The Nitrogen Fix* shows a different sort of human family, the Fyns, returning by raft to an unusually changed Boston Bay area after an expedition of gathering. We learn that one of the products they gathered is the copper harvested from acid oceans by zeowhales. Far more unusual, however, is the dramatically changed environment of Earth, the only world known to the Fyns. We learn that the story is really a story of a scientific blunder—a fix or predicament—on a grand scale. Because of the energy crisis sometime in their own near future, scientists apparently began the biological engineering of microbes in order to make agriculture more productive. A process had been developed for accelerating the "fixing" (removing) of free nitrogen from the atmosphere into soil-bound nitrogen compounds. By the time of the novel, this process has produced, presumably in addition to more nitrogen fertilizer at first, truly catastrophic results. [As a teacher of chemistry and general science at Milton Academy, an exclusive prep school near Boston, Clement is particularly able to analyze and describe these results].

The oceans have become solutions of nitric acid, weak but still able to yellow the skin. Numerous nitrogen compounds in the new environment behave explosively and unpredictably. Worst of all, only a trace of free oxygen remains in the atmosphere. Plant life in the open has evolved to a nitrogen-based life that produces its energy by reducing nitrates, often explosively. Other nitrogen life forms, large and small, including the most fascinating of alien species, make use of this chemical reaction of reduction, rather than oxidation, to produce their energy needed for life. In reality, Clement knows that enough energy to sustain life can be produced by this chemical process of reduction, for some microscopic life forms do currently live on Earth using this process; he reasons that there could be enough nitrogen compounds on a larger scale to provide the necessary vital energy. In his extrapolation, the only animal life forms remaining on Earth that still depend on oxidation to live are the small colonies of humans who carefully produce breathable air from plants in underground cities. A few nomads live as outcasts in the open air of the nitrogen atmosphere. And one element of the story follows the primitive technology of survival in the open used by the nomad Fyn family.

The fascinating alien nitrogen-based species, in some ways, dominates the action of the novel more than the humans do. The prime motivation for this alien species, called the "Observers" by Clement, is simply curiosity. They seem to be the archetypal scientists, or seekers after knowledge for its own sake, but with a strange difference. The species has been drawn to Earth by the nitrogen buildup in the atmosphere, and we learn that the species has seen the same process take place on over a dozen planets within the memory of the Observer representatives on Earth. Actually, the Observers are a hive species with a common memory. Each individual unit, of which two figure in the novel, can share total communication and memory with the entire species, once contact with any other unit has been made. The contact for communication appears, to the humans in the novel, to be similar to sexual contact. Further, direct and immediate communication of this sort contradicts Clement's belief in the gradual and indirect accumulation of knowledge. Thus the pooling of knowledge that the aliens do by touching makes them seem even more alien. It is definitely not sexual touching because the species has no sex differences, and reproduction for them is by parthenogenesis. They are simply driven by curiosity and they possess the ability to achieve immediate and telepathiclike communication. These strange and helpful characters, then, allow Clement to raise the question of how we know what we know.

As the surviving humans in the novel struggle among themselves and, also, struggle to understand the peculiar aliens that have come to Earth, the most helpful Observer puzzles over human ways of knowing. The Fyns have named him "Bones" since he has no skeleton; he is a large, likeable, and eternally curious character. Clement writes about Bones pondering these issues:

> Bones was fascinated. Psychology was another totally new field to a mind which has not only never met another intelligent species until now, but had never encountered a different mind in its own. This crowd of *individuals*, cut off from each other except through crude and time consuming code symbols, was a revelation—a brand new field of knowledge—indeed, a whole set of such fields. It was obvious that the incomplete and distorted picture of the universe transmitted by words would have fantastically unpredictable effects on those minds; the code symbols themselves

would probably take the place of the reality they were supposed
to transmit much of the time. . . .

It would not occur to Bones for a long time that the Observer's
sensory impressions were just as much a coded representation of
reality as were human words. So were the molecular patterns
which recorded those impressions, and passed them from one
Observer unit to another. The species was a good scientist, but
not yet a philosopher.

Clement seems to be interested not only in the nitrogen-based
physiology and alien appearance of this character, both of which
are fantastic extrapolations from his plausible starting point about
nitrogen-based life, but also in the puzzles about how we know
things that the character encounters. Even though the Observer
species can communicate by direct chemical interaction, with
the droll analogy to human sexual contact, knowledge for the
species is still indirect and thus uncertain. Clement suggests, in
other words, that regardless of what symbol system we use to
perceive and to communicate, we can never overcome some limits on what we can know about the universe. Later he will have
the curious Observers discover a variation in the pattern, when
a means is found during the course of the novel to reverse the
process of nitrogen buildup in the atmosphere. The species has
never seen a reversal of the process on any of the other planets
they have been drawn to visit.

Along with the curious Observers, the reader wants to discover
what really happened on Earth to cause the nitrogen buildup in
the atmosphere. But most of the surviving humans are less curious, because they mistrust science and the experimental
method. For example, the Fyn family, whom we get to know
best, depend on a set of values and practice the reverse of what
we know as the scientific method. They are self-reliant nomads,
and their family name reminds us of the resourcefulness of Huck
Finn, but they are afraid to try anything new. Custom and habit
are far better guides to action for them than independent thinking. Following the ecological diaster that destroyed most oxygen-
based life on the surface of the Earth, words like "experiment"
and "invent" became dirty words. One of the main actions of the
novel is the gradual discovery by the humans that innovative

thinking can be a useful tool and a way of knowing. On the one hand, Clement explores through the species of the Observers the limits to knowledge even in the direct communication of thought. On the other hand, Clement creates human characters who must learn gradually to overcome a deep antiscientific bias. In these details, then, the novel would seem to be very skeptical about the possibilities in any method of knowing things.

Nevertheless, both the humans and the Observers do learn, and progress is promised by the end of the novel, even if it does come indirectly and from one of the most unlikely places. The possibility for a reversal of the process of nitrogen buildup comes from the very culprit itself—science, in particular, biological engineering. Microbes are being developed by gene manipulation that will release free oxygen from nitrogen compounds back into the atmosphere. Although it is not clear how long these processes will take, the ultimate hope is that open air photosynthesis and blue skies (rather than yellow) may return to Earth. If that should happen, the Observer species would move on to learn from another nitrogen environment. But it is unlikely that they would find such a paradoxical species of mixed creatures as they have encountered on Earth.

The most dramatic mix of all has to do with the secret experiments to develop the new microbes. Though it may be seen simply as an extension of Clement's notion of accumulating more knowledge from partial knowledge and even from mistakes, the most profound reversal of method in the novel is the unlikely origin of this experimentation. Work progressed slowly, but it is the only possible hope of returning Earth to an oxygen-based habitable environment. The work is done, not by the Fyns, with whom the reader identifies most, but by a group of young "oxygen wasters" from one of the underground cities, who are violent in behavior and fanatically wrong in many of their hypotheses. This group of Hillers, or city dwellers, who "invent" the new microbe, believe passionately that the Observer species has destroyed the earth's atmosphere. In other words, the truly rational creatures in this story are the Observers with their oneness and compulsive curiosity who are yet blind to the possibility of change (no planet in their experience has ever reversed the process of nitrogen buildup); whereas potentially beneficial change and progress is brought about by a group of irrational men who are patently wrong about the past. In between are the Fyns, who gradually learn from both.

Finally, the Observers seem disinterested. They are truly objective, curious about whatever develops around them, with perhaps no real ability to change anything. At the end of the book, they are helpful in protecting the rebels who are developing the proper mechanism to return free oxygen to the Earth, even though the Observers will have to leave once this change takes place. Continually in the narrative, the pure reason of the Observers is compared to the confusion, ignorance, and violence of the humans. When the group of humans who have seemed the most confused, ignorant, and violent do invent the new microbe, Clement's ironic twists about assumptions about knowledge are complete. The reversals and ambiguities, however, that Clement has carefully built into the situations of *The Nitrogen Fix* are not new to his work, though they may be the most complex.

Clement's early novelette, "Impediment" (1942), is also about how we know things. It deals with language as a means of communication, as opposed to direct communication through something like telepathy. A crew of strange aliens, who look like huge moths, have landed on Earth and are interested in communicating with the intelligent human inhabitants they find. The only problem is that the mothmen communicate by the direct perception of nerve configurations. They don't have to touch like the Observers, but they read minds. Thus the human, Kirk, whom their spokescreature, Talker, gets to know, must actually teach the system of symbols we call language to the mothmen in order to understand them. Kirk cannot read Talker's mind although Kirk's thoughts are easily perceived by the aliens. Clement's title, then, is ironic in several ways. First of all, Kirk has an "impediment" to communication because he lacks telepathy. Secondly, the conversations between Kirk and Talker develop hesitantly, like a speech therapist to a mute, although by the conclusion of their relatively short association they converse fairly well. But most drastic is Talker's basic impediment. He will never be a creature who is comfortable with language because the basic communication mode of his species is telepathic. Thus the mothmen have the real speech "impediment."

What bothers Clement about the telepathic, or direct, communication of information (whether it is the mothmen's telepathy here or the hive memory of the Observers activated by touching) is that it is too perfect, and thus closed. He prefers the general purpose code system of a language. Language must be learned gradually, and there is always the danger of mistranslation from speaker to speaker. Even when a speaker speaks to himself or herself internally, there is the possibility of misunderstanding and mistake, but a general purpose code system allows continual new combinations and hence the chance for continual new knowledge. The greatest irony is that in an impediment, such as partial knowledge, there is strength. On the other hand, the absolutist, or nondoubter, such as a mothman telepath, has the largest impediment. Even Clement's sophomoric language in this early story (he wrote it while he was still a Harvard undergraduate) captures the irony well. Perhaps the finest example comes near the conclusion when Kirk communicates to Talker his realization, finally, of where the greatest impediment in communication lies and, ironically, where the strength in language lies:

> Your people all "think" alike—so far as either of us is able to tell what thought is. The patterns you broadcast are mutually intelligible to members of your race, but not to me, because you have received those waves from others of your kind from earliest childhood, and I am a stranger. But my people do not communicate in that fashion. . . . The activity that occurs in our brains is never directly transmitted to other brains—it is first "coded" and then broadcast. . . . From birth, each [human] brain is isolated, can be reached only through the means of communication natural to us; there is no reason that all should develop alike.

Thus, knowledge for Clement is always partial and always accumulating, rather than directly revealed and complete. The way to thrive in such a system is to collect many bits of information, to get a lot of cooperation. Clement has written a whole group of novels about humans and aliens cooperating, in which limitations and even mistakes in reasoning contribute to what we ultimately know. In a sense, this is a Baconian solution to the limitations of knowledge and probably the best known characteristic of Clement's work. He creates a great variety of alien life forms and alien environments—a variety of observers—because one way to build up a store of partial knowledge, if it cannot be gotten by direct revelation, is to make use of a lot of curious and potentially intelligent beings. Another way is to imagine a variety of conditions, because as things change, more can be learned about what drives the changes. Scientists call such speculations thought experiments. Clement is a virtuoso with both kinds of extrapolation in science fiction.

The alien creatures in his fiction are almost always curious as well as crafty, hence potential learners. The accumulation of a tremendous amount of data from different points results. His best-known aliens are the caterpillarlike Mesklinites from his classic *Mission of Gravity*, who shrewdly learn to overcome their fear of falling. This is no small accomplishment since the variable and incredibly high gravity on the planet Mesklin has resulted in evolution of life very close to the ground. The Mesklinites even learn from their human visitors the physics of flight. At the same time of course, Clement's reader, along with the human explorers, learn a lot about the conditions on Mesklin.

Clement's stories are peopled with human explorers who use intelligent natives to help them learn, and clever natives like the Mesklinites, who use humans in the same way. Clement envisions peaceful and constructive cooperation between scientifically-minded life forms throughout the universe. For example, the Observers in *The Nitrogen Fix* are never aggressive. Only the small band of headstrong Hillers, who discover the saving microbe, want to fight. Clement portrays very little tooth and fang competition for living space nor much space opera aggression. The universe seems large enough for all, and even when mistakes such as the nitrogen imbalance cause catastrophe, with luck and skill Clement's characters manipulate the environment to correct matters. Some of Clement's fiction is modeled after the detective story, and a few of his characters, both human and alien, are criminals, but crime is generally overcome in these stories by careful reasoning.

The universe itself is the really dangerous antagonist. Nature is full of variety and unpredictable conditions, but the more we know about how it changes, the more prepared we are to consider the probable outcome of even more varied conditions. Clement's fiction demonstrates this through his choice of setting. He uses imagination, creating a variety of planetary environments to consider more bits of information and to accumulate more knowledge. His novels are the most extreme form of thought experiment. In fact, the use of stories to contribute to how we know things about the universe is very close to gaining knowledge from our mistakes, because stories are fictions or "lies." Such literary sophistication is seldom discussed by Clement, but I think it is central to his approach.

Clement's most representative type of story is the tale of exploration of unusual and varied planetary environments. Immediately before *Mission of Gravity* in the early 1950s, he started the pattern with *Iceworld*, a novel about the exploration of the planet Earth from an alien point of view. The story explores the puzzles in the environment of Earth (the "iceworld") from the point of view of alien scientists from the planet Sarr, where the temperature range is high enough and the atmospheric pressure low enough so that most matter is in the gaseous state. There is some irony in this reversal as the reader looks at the physical characteristics of his own familiar world through the eyes of creatures who marvel at the possibility of intelligent life, or any organic activity at all, on a planet with such peculiar atmosphere conditions. Clement's reversal, however, emphasizes less the irony of difference and more the sheer excitement of discovery. As much as any of the long fiction to follow, *Iceworld* is an exercise in the gradual uncovering of the biochemistry and atmospheric makeup of a planet. But in this case the information is the familiar data about free and active oxygen, about atmospheric pressure equal to what physicists call one atmosphere, about boiling points of liquids, and especially about our prime liquid, water, which the aliens call hydrogen oxide.

Perhaps after he had gone through this exercise in *Iceworld* of presenting this data from high school science, Clement could then move on to the more speculative thought experiments in planetary environments of his later novels. His next novel after

Iceworld was *Mission of Gravity*, and then in close succession came *Cycle of Fire* (1957), *Close to Critical* (1964), which was serialized in the later 1950s, and finally another Mesklinite novel, *Star Light* (1971). By the time of *Star Light*, Clement had formulated the notion of an energy crisis in the life cycle of all inhabitable planets and was also writing fiction about biological engineering referred to earlier in this essay. Although it is fascinating work to follow the thought experiments and to describe the planetary environments as well as their alien life forms, the central point in Clement's work is the variety of life forms and physical details. The following passage from *Star Light* which refers explicitly to Clement's conception of the Energy Crisis also hints at the number of these details. One of the chief administrators in the human exploration team that is using Mesklinites to study the huge planetary body Dhrawn (Mesklinites here also are using the humans to broaden their own knowledge) outlines the scheme:

> You know as well as I do that in the very small volume of space within five parsecs of Sol, with only seventy-four known stars and about two hundred sunless planets, what we have found in the way of intelligence: twenty races at about our own stage of development, safely past their Energy Crisis; eight, including Tenebra [the planet in *Close to Critical*] and Mesklin, which haven't met it yet; eight which failed to pass it and are extinct; three which failed but have some hope of recovery; every one of them, remember, within a hundred thousand years of that key point in their history, one way or the other! That's in spite of the fact that the planets range in age from Panesh's nine billion years or so to Tenebra's maybe a tenth of that.

Unlike the works of Frank Herbert or other space opera series, the variety of worlds in Clement's work is never made into a complete system. Some of the planets, such as Panesh, he has written no fiction about; he simply seems most interested in variety and difference.

In this short review of some of his other fiction, we can see that *The Nitrogen Fix* is a consistent and even anticipated fulfillment in Clement's writing. In the novel, he explores a drastically changed planetary environment on Earth. Aliens participate and help in the exploration. The drastic change in the environment has apparently been produced by an attempt to deal with the energy crisis. Earth is at the crossroads between extinction or survival. Finally, a major preoccupation within the narrative itself has to do with how we know things. The ironies and ambiguities in these methods of knowing, seem deepest and most significant in this recent bit of partial knowledge that we know as Clement's latest novel.

Just prior to the introduction of the terminology of modern chemistry, the word for nitrogen gas was "azote," meaning "not live." This was the chemist Antoine Lavoisier's term because in his experiments he found that he could not support life with this gas he had isolated. *The Nitrogen Fix*, in a sense, is about the ambiguities in the relationship between life and death. The most interesting characters in the book are the nitrogen-based Observers. As we have seen, they are helpful in protecting the rebels who are developing the proper solution to return an oxygen-based environment to Earth. Thus not only does the solution come from a group that is mistaken about many things, including the nature of the Observers, but also the nitrogen, or "death"-based life assists in bringing back the vitality of free oxygen to Earth's atmosphere.

A further ambiguity in the story is the Golden Age/Iron Age vision of progress. The notion of lost Golden Ages appears in the novel almost by surprise. It deepens and enriches a pathos in Clement's work that is associated, I believe, with the death/life ambiguity, one that is seen most effectively in his earlier work, *Cycle of Fire*. But the reader does not expect it. We do not absolutely need to know what enzyme accelerates the oxygen fixation reaction in the originally engineered microbes. The narrative hints at this bit of information often until Clement reveals, near the end of the book, that the real culprit is gold. Just before the name of the metal is revealed, one of the Observers explains why it has always seemed strange to the scientific curiosity of its species that the widespread distribution of gold should immediately precede the ecological change to nitrogen life. In the case of Earth, this sounds like a grand ecological disaster following an age of gold, a nitrogen age following an oxygen age, a dark age following a scientific age. Here is part of the Observer's speech:

> I have not been able to learn why it [gold] is so widespread in every planet's crust. It is one of the standing mysteries, which presents itself on world after world. It is a highly unreactive metal, which I would expect to find uncombined and highly localized. It should *not* be so thoroughly spread through a planet's soil and crust that a microbe can count on finding enough of its atoms whenever it needs them for its personal chemistry. One hypothesis is that a scientific race used and scattered it, but there has been no way to tell; I have never found a use for it myself, except in the most limited quantities in the laboratory.

Once again the character of the Observers comes across as that of the pure rationalist, with no passion for gold, whereas true science progresses in a mixed and uncertain manner.

Thus, ideas that I think have been latent in Clement's work all along are brought to explicit expression in this novel where gold is the culprit and where progress and the solution to problems is complex. The mythic Iron Age was certainly a degenerate time compared to the glories of the Golden Age, but paradoxically, progress can take place in an Iron Age—even more so than in a Golden Age, when development is more or less static because of the utopian conditions. Clement continually compares the pure reason of the Observers to the confusion of the humans, but the humans do invent the new microbe, and progress always occurs in an Iron Age when less than golden means are used. Clement's version of this paradox has always been his belief that limited, partial knowledge is the best source of accumulating knowledge and thus of progress. Here the paradox is made more explicit in this latest of his stories by the fact that the antiscientific attitudes and the abhorrence of experimentation eventually gives way to what will be the life-giving solution even in the nitrogen age after the catastrophe. The death-life of nitrogen will eventually lead to the vitality of real life, life as we oxygen creatures know it, on Earth again.

Carl Yoke

ROGER ZELAZNY'S BOLD NEW MYTHOLOGIES

That Roger Zelazny's writing is heavily mythic is generally known. Some critics, in fact, have even accused him of attempting to translate whole bodies of myth into science fiction and have thus implied that his major, and perhaps only, reason for writing was to restate particular myths. Nothing, of course, could be further from the truth. Indeed, Zelazny uses myth in his stories, more so in his earlier work than in his later, but always with a specific purpose in mind. And he has never sacrificed the integrity of his own story for that of a myth he has chosen to use. On the contrary, he adapts myth to his stories, often with disturbing results for readers who expect the story to resolve itself through a familiar form.

Zelazny's reasons for relying so heavily on myth, I believe, are relatively easy to explain. First, when he began to write seriously for publication, he naturally turned to materials in which he was well-versed. Mythology happened to be one of them. He began reading it at an early age in its truncated form, as fairy tale, and this led him quickly into folklore and myth. Second, he has always been an inveterate experimenter. He has stated both publicly and privately that he tries not to write formula stories, that he looks for new angles, new perspectives, new techniques. This attitude has led him to seek different effects in his continuing effort to explore the infinity of relationships that can and do exist between people. And the myths provided him with a gold mine of recurring themes, characters, and plots to enrich his own stories.

Zelazny's writing is also notable for its superb characterization. He has a deep understanding of human nature; he is very sensitive to the needs, desires, and goals of people. The characters he creates, despite their larger-than-life physical qualities, are always psychologically realistic. So are his themes. We encounter them in our daily affairs: greed, pride, ambition, revenge, guilt, betrayal, love, growth, renewal. Though they are scaled up to fit Zelazny's science fiction worlds, they are nonetheless the emotions and experiences that create the very fabric of human existence.

The effect of this combination of psychological realism and mythology is recognized by Theodore Sturgeon in his "Introduction" to *Four for Tomorrow*:

> Zelazny's stories are fabulous. . . . And it has come to me over the years that the greatness of literature and the importance of literary entities (Captain Ahab, Billy Budd, Hamlet, Job, Uriah Heep) really lies in this fabulous quality. One may ponderously call them Jungian archetypes, but one recognizes them, and/or their situational predicaments, in one's daily contacts with this landlord, that employer, and one's dearly beloved. A fable says more than it says, is bigger than its own parameters. Zelazny always says more than he says; all his yarns have applications, illuminate truths, donate to the reader tools (and sometimes weapons) with which he was not equipped before, and for which, he can find daily uses, quite outside the limits of the story.

Zelazny's stories are fabulous, and one of the primary techniques he uses to create this quality is his manipulation of what we might loosely classify as mythic elements. By adapting the symbols, characters, plots, and themes of myth, including specific archetypal figures or historic figures who have taken on the trappings of myth, he not only adds dimension and scope to his own characters but to his themes as well. More specifically, he adapts them to shape his own characters, to deepen their significance, to symbolize their points of view, to help structure a work, to set the moral values of a story, and to deepen the significance of a theme. A close examination of some of his best stories will illustrate the result of his experimentation.

The best example of his use of a mythological character to

shape one of his own occurs in his award-winning novelette, "The Doors of His Face, the Lamps of His Mouth." In it, the protagonist, a baitman (who tracks and catches sea creatures in Venusian oceans) named Carlton Davits, is patterned after Job. Both men, for example, suffer from the fault of pride, and though neither is arrogant, each is so egotistical that it blocks him from the insight necessary to his psychological growth. Both initially hold high status in their respective cultures, both fall from that state, both are tested, both are left physically scarred from the testing, and both eventually mature.

Job's wealth and status are verified in verse 1:3 where it is reported that he owns 7,000 sheep, 3,000 camels, 500 she-asses, and 500 yoke of oxen. Moreover, he has "a very great household" and is "the greatest of the men of the east." Davits's wealth and status are established by the fact that he once purchased "Tensquare," an atomic-powered ship the size of a football field simply to indulge his desire to fish for an "Ikky," a Venusian leviathan similar to the extinct Earth *plesiosaur*, which had never before been caught. Only a few of the wealthiest and most influential men can afford such a luxury.

Both men fall from their high estates. Job loses all of his material possessions and his sons and daughters are killed when a high wind topples their house on them. After a psychological trauma, Davits goes bankrupt, becomes an alcoholic drifter, and is divorced by his wife, Jean. The causes of the respective falls, however, differ. God permits Satan to test Job; the cause of his fall is outside himself. By contrast, Davits's fall is self-generated, the result of his overconfidence. But each falls because he is not mature enough to handle failure, whether real or imagined, and because he is prevented from insight into his own peculiar circumstances by his pride.

Both men are tested, Job by Satan and Davits by fear. In addition to losing their possessions, each man finds his most meaningful personal relationships destroyed and sustains physical injury. Job suffers "sore boils from the soles of his feet unto his crown." Davits suffers partial hemiplegia from his first encounter with an "Ikky" and later receives bad wounds in a diving accident from the screw of a ship called the *Dolphin*.

Though it is clear that Zelazny draws Davits from Job, Davits is not simply a translation of him. Zelazny has very carefully differentiated his protagonist from the Biblical sufferer by heavily psychologizing him. The result is to make Davits more acceptable to contemporary readers and thus more believable. Using the dynamics of Jungian psychology, Zelasny makes his story a dramatization of a man's search for balance in his personality. At the psychological level, Ikky is a symbol of Jung's subconscious system, called "the Shadow," which manifests the energy of our animal natures, and the encounter between Davits and Ikky mirrors the development of a strong persona to counteract the power of the shadow.

In another award-winning novelette, " . . . And Call Me Conrad," later expanded and retitled *This Immortal*, Zelazny adds a variation to his technique of linking the protagonist to a mythical character. He clusters several mythic and historic identities with the qualities he wishes to emphasize in his protagonist around a central core of personality, in this particular case, Conrad. The clustering tends to strengthen and emphasize the qualities the identities share through a kind of echo effect, and thus to imbue Conrad with an overlaid and symbolic significance. In *This Immortal*, for instance, Conrad is linked either directly or by innuendo to Hephaestus, Karaghiosis, Lord Hades, Cronos, Papa Legba, Dionysius, and others. Though each identity does not possess all of the relevant qualities to the same degree, they collectively exhibit three characteristics which Zelazny wants the reader eventually to identify with Conrad: caretaker of the underworld, fertility figure, and instrument of change.

The Greek god Hephaestus (known as Vulcan to the Romans) is never mentioned by name in the book, but is introduced into it, instead, by an allusion to the ballad of the limping boy who breaks the back of Themocles after wrestling him for three days. Hephaestus is the basis for the physical description of Conrad. In the myths about him and Vulcan, he is usually pictured as lame, ugly, and incredibly strong. So is Conrad, and there are other parallels. Both have been rejected by their parents and left in the elements to die. Both are destined to try to overthrow their superiors. One of the Hephaestus myths, as reported by John Pinset, predicts that he will try to overthrow Zeus, and Conrad, when he was known as Karaghiosis, tried to overthrow the Vegans by means of a revolutionary group known as Radpol. He later succeeds, in a figurative way, when he is chosen to literally inherit the Earth by Vegan Cort Myshtigo.

Hephaestus and Conrad both stand as patrons to art and culture. As the god of creative fire, Hephaestus is regarded as the patron of artisans, and as Commissioner of Arts, Monuments, and Archives, Conrad's job is to preserve and restore Earth's art treasures and culture. Both, too, are either directly or indirectly associated with the underworld. Because he is a smith and thereby linked to fire, Hephaestus recalls the Christian myth of Hell. Conrad becomes the caretaker of a devastated, radioactive Earth, an island culture because the continents are still hot, a figurative Hell. Finally, both are associated with fertility. Hephaestus is married to Aphrodite, the goddess of love and beauty, and one myth tells the story of how he fell madly in love with Athena. She visited his forge one day, he pursued her only to be rejected, and in his desire, he brushed against her. Disgusted, she rubbed off the sperm with a piece of cloth, which she threw to the ground. The earth thus fertilized bore a child named Erichthonius, who founded the dynasty of Attican kings that eventually produced the great house of Theseus. And once Conrad inherits the Earth, his major function becomes the restoration of fertility to his devastated planet.

A second example is found in Conrad's association with the Haitian god, Papa Legba. He is introduced into the novel when Conrad takes some of the other characters, Cort, Hassan, Ellen, Dos Santos, and Diane to a voodoo ceremony at a *hounfor*, a mystery house where such rites are held. Papa Legba's roots go back to Dahomey, where he was one of the slaves of the old gods. His primary function is to act as intermediary between them and man. Thus, sacrifices are made to him first so he will open the gates between the sacred and profane. William Seabrook's *The Magic Island*, which Zelazny alludes to in the novel, describes Papa Legba as "the Priapus of Dahomey, the god of generation and fecundity." Seabrook also links Papa Legba to Pan:

> Other signs of wonder also became manifest. Into this little temple
> lost among the mountains came in answer to goat-cry girl-cry the

Shaggy Immortal One of a thousand names whom the Greeks
called Pan. The goat's lingam became erect and rigid, the points
of the girl's breasts became visibly hardened and were outlined
sharply pressing against the coarse, thin, tight-drawn shift that was
her only garment.

While the fertility element is obvious in the above quote, the
link to the underworld is subtle. To the Greeks, Pan was both
a shepherd and a fertility deity, one of a group of chthonic gods
called *daemon*. For them, a *daemon* was always bearded, horned,
and held in high respect. It was the Christians who made them
infamous by linking them to the Devil. According to Jeffrey Burton Russell, the impact of Pan iconography on the Christian concept of the Devil was enormous:

> The Devil is frequently described as taking animal forms, most
> commonly that of the goat. The root of the similarity is the asso-
> ciation of the Devil with the chthonic fertility deities, who were
> rejected by the Christians as demons along with the other pagan
> gods and who were particularly feared because of their association
> with the wilderness and with sexual frenzy. Sexual passion, which
> suspends reason and easily leads to excess, was alien to both the
> rationalism of the Greeks and the asceticism of the Christians; a
> god of sexuality could easily be assimilated to the principle of
> evil. The association of the chthonic with both sex and the un-
> derworld, and hence with death, sealed the union.

Aspects of both fertility god and caretaker of the underworld
emerge in Papa Legba, and by association, in Conrad. Analyses
of the other figures to which Conrad is linked yields similar
information, and the collection of identities deepens his
significance.

Yet another mythic technique that Zelazny uses is to make a
field of related images and references stand symbolically for a
character's point of view. His grandest experiment in this vein
occurs in his Nebula Award winning novella "He Who Shapes,"
later expanded and retitled *The Dream Master*. In that novel,
Zelazny carefully constructs two symbolic clusters which are
worked through the story and which come to be identified with
the respective views of its two principal characters. The clusters

derive from Arthurian lore and the Scandinavian myth of
ragnarok.

The Arthurian material is associated with Eileen Shallot, a
blind-from-birth psychiatrist seeking sight. She is highly intelligent, very strong willed, and neurotic. The cluster of references
symbolizes both the quality of her mind and her view of the
world, which is idealistic, romantic, and chivalric. The shattering
of this perspective during neuroparticipation therapy radically
alters her concept of self and this, in turn, releases her trapped
psychic energy with such force that it draws Charles Render, the
novel's protagonist, into her madness.

Arthurian references abound in the novel from the first appearance of Eileen. Her surname, Shallot, immediately calls to
mind Lord Tennyson's poem "The Lady of Shalott," whose
sources are Arthurian. Her initial meeting with Render is marked
by a suit of armor standing beside their table at a restaurant
called "The Partridge and Scalpel," and there are many similarities of both situation and character between Eileen and Tennyson's Lady. Many of *The Dream Master*'s symbols, such as the
willow, the river, and the color gray derive from the poem.

As with the Arthurian material, the *ragnarok,* or "twilight of
the gods" myth comes to represent the mind and world view of
Render. He is an ego-centered and self-deceived psychiatrist,
whose technique for treating neurosis is by entering his patients'
dreams and reshaping them. Theoretically, through a series of
controlled fantasies, he gradually creates new and psychologically healthy personalities for his patients. This is accomplished
by a machine called the "ro-womb."

Render recognizes Eileen's idealistic point of view but believes, in his supreme egotism, that he can balance it with perceptions of reality. This, he feels, will be sufficient to offset the
inherent dangers of dealing with sight-trauma. But he fails to
recognize his own vulnerability, and eventually, Eileen, supported by an enormous surge of psychic energy, takes control of
the final fantasy from him. He tries to show her a view of Win-
chester Cathedral, which he had just seen on a trip to England,
only to have her recreate the Tristam and Isolde myth. It is a
logical development since that myth is an integral part of the
Arthurian material.

The *ragnarok* myth is a story of inevitable doom. No matter what the gods do, they are fated to fall. Their destruction marks the end of the created world, and by his association with the myth, Render too is consigned to fail. To make the idea more believable to contemporary readers, Zelazny locks Render into a pattern of psychological determinism which leads him to destruction. The combination of his pride and his vulnerability, brought about by the neurotic complex generated by the death of his wife and young daughter nine years earlier, create the necessary psychological prods to force him to his destiny.

As with Eileen and the Lady of Shallot, there are parallels between Render and Odin, and elements of the *ragnarok* are worked into the fabric of the story from the beginning. In the myth, one of the signals of the onset of the gods' destruction is a mighty winter that will bring three years of unrelieved cold and snow. Zelazny adapts this to the novel by filling scenes with images of winter, which are, in turn, associated with death. Yet another signal of the *ragnarok* is the swallowing of the moon by a wolf. Render fears dogs and in the middle of the last fantasy, Fenris, a giant wolf and enemy of the gods, appears to eat the corpses of wife and daughter. At the beginning of the sequence, Zelazny states that the Fenris swallowed the moon. The image has a double significance in the context of the novel. Since Odin is fated to be swallowed by Fenris, it first signals that Render's end is near, but it also signals that Eileen, with whom Zelazny has associated the traditional symbol of the moon, has lost her own sanity.

The adaptation of the myth is superb. In Snorri Sturluson's version of the *ragnarok* in *The Prose Edda*, there are two wolves: Fenris and another, named Moon-Hound. Fenris actually swallows the sun, and Moon-Hound the moon, but two wolves in Zelazny's story would have complicated the symbolism unnecessarily. Zelazny has identified the moon with Eileen, primarily through the photoelectric sensing device that she wears on her forehead and which is often described as "moonlike." The association is appropriate, for the moon is an extrinsic symbol of femininity produced by ages of association with such deities as Astarte, Ishtar, and Semele.

By bringing the Arthurian and Scandinavian symbol complexes together in the final dream sequence, Zelazny dramatizes the conflict between the points of view of the two principal characters in his novel. And, in this particular case, he is also letting the myths structure the novel to some degree. The ultimate failure of Render is the working out of the fate of Odin, with whom he is identified. It is reinforced by the Tristam and Isolde myth, which also predicts the destruction of Eileen.

A better example of the use of myth to structure a work is found in Zelazny's Hugo winner, *Lord of Light*. It also provides another example of the use of a mythological figure to structure one of Zelazny's own. The book's protagonist, Mahasamatman, or Sam, is broadly patterned after Gotama Sakyamuni, the historical Buddha. The events of the Buddha's life are paralleled in Sam's. Both leave home, family, and high estate; both achieve a kind of enlightenment; both undergo nirvana; both reform the existing religion and society; and both liberate mankind from the constraints of widespread oppression. Zelazny's treatment of these events within the world he creates for his story is highly imaginative.

The broad structuring of the novel is assured once Zelazny commits Sam to assume the same mission that the historical Buddha undertook. As described by Joseph Politella, it was:

> ... to restore to Hinduism an eclecticism which had become too narrow; to re-interpret, as the old Rajputs knew them, the twin doctrines of Karma-Rebirth; and once more to point out that the cause of all human misery is the mistaking of the unreal for the true and everlasting.... These were the truths which the Brahmans had apparently lost; or which, holding for themselves, had kept the enlightenment from the other castes, thus causing them to fall into blindness and ignorance by sheer neglect—or worse, by spiritual pride and insolence.

Moreover, Buddha decried "the tyrannical domination of the priestly caste," punctured and deflated "the whole system of ceremonial salvation," opposed "an exclusive spirituality based on caste segregation," showed "the futility of mechanical prayers with penances and indulgences," and reestablished "once more the teaching that spiritual growth may be guided, but it is individual and personal." Sam accomplishes these same objectives within the world of the story.

To assure Sam's credibility as a savior and to expand his significance, Zelazny links him not only with the historical Buddha, but also with Kalki and Maitreya, the Hindu and Buddhist names for the buddha-who-is-yet-to-come. In both religions, the appearance of this buddha signals the end of the current age. Significantly, Maitreya is also known as the "Lord of Light" and will save mankind with his love. Zelazny condenses qualities of the three buddhas into the character of Sam, taking from each those aspects which best fit the novel.

Yet another use that Zelazny finds for myth is to set the moral values of a story. The best example of this occurs in his "Amber" novels. The story itself is set against Zelazny's "form and chaos" philosophy, which is itself without moral value. Chaos appears in almost every mythology and has ambivalent value because it appears at both the beginning and end of time. It is often felt to be bad because it represents the destruction of the world, but it is good in the sense that it represents a return to or a recreation of primeval power and creativity. In Zelazny's cosmology, form is the power opposed to chaos, but both forces are necessary to the progress of the universe and both are innate to each living being. Moral value is an attribute of consciousness and intelligence. Since form and chaos are morally neutral, it then becomes necessary to establish moral value by some other means. Zelazny accomplishes this in the Amber books by two principal symbol clusters, one of which represents good, the other, evil. At the center of the first cluster is the unicorn, standing for Christ. At the center of the other is Brand, standing for the Devil.

Though it passed through a strange and complex evolution, the unicorn eventually became associated with Christ and came to have a standard appearance: ". . . a pure white animal, vaguely equine but smaller than a horse, with goat's beard and cloven hoofs and the spiralled horn." This is the description Zelazny uses in the novels, and he uses it to establish the moral value of good. The unicorn traditionally possessed two qualities which support this contention. It had water-conning ability—that is, it dipped its horn into poisoned water to absorb the poison so that other good animals might drink—and an appetite for snakes, traditional symbols of the devil in Christian mythology. Another feature found in many unicorn tales is that a precious stone, usually a ruby, grew at the base of its horn. In one version, Wolfram von Eschenbach's *Parzifal*, there is even a reference to the unicorn's ruby as one of several medicines used to heal the wound of Anfortas, who is described as "King of the Grail."

The similarity between that legend and the appearance of a unicorn wearing the Jewel of Judgment, a red stone, near the end of *The Courts of Chaos* is unmistakable. Moreover, she delivers the stone to Random, the protagonist's half brother, thus declaring him the successor to Oberon, the dead king, and metaphorically curing the wound of the new king and providing the means for restoring the land. The connection between the unicorn and the Grail in the *Parzifal* is logical, for both the unicorn legends and the grail quests are Christ-related, and the Amber novels contain a prototypic grail quest spread through the five books. This material, along with other references, supports the unicorn as a symbol of good.

A similar cluster of images and references is used to create evil in the novels. It is focused through the character of Brand, another half brother of Corwin, the protagonist. Several signs mark Brand as a symbol of the Devil and evil. First, he has red hair, and in European folklore red-haired people were thought to be in league with the devil because they were believed to be members of witch cults. Also, the word "brand" suggests fire, and fire, of course, is associated with the Devil in Christianity. In *The Courts of Chaos*, the last of the novels. Brand often appears concurrently with flashing red light, clearly a mimicking of Hell's fire. Brand is generally associated with the color red, which is itself associated with the Devil. Russell writes:

> The reddish glow of hellfire and the reddish tint of land scorched by fire or by an intemperate sun seem to have produced (together with blood) the association of redness with evil that persists in modern conceptions of the Devil's appearance.

Also, Brand tempts Corwin with power during the journey that Corwin makes to Chaos to deliver the Jewel of Judgment and thus save the universe which is already collapsing around them.

The temptation is reminiscent of many such scenes in the stories of Christianity and other religions. Moreover, in the lore of the Tarot (and the novels are full of Tarot imagery), the Devil tries to tempt the Fool during the Fool's journey, and Corwin is clearly identified with the Fool in the books. Finally, the Devil is the polar opposite of the Archangel in Key 14 of the Tarot and that Archangel is Michael. In Revelations, Michael is identified as the Archangel who, with a band of loyal angels, successfully warred with Lucifer, and Corwin is referred to as an "Archangel" by a dark stranger he encounters in a cave as he seeks refuge on his way to Chaos from a storm that is destroying all form before it. It is Zelazny's version of Armageddon. The pattern fits too well to assume anything other than that Corwin is linked with good and Brand with the Devil and evil.

Other characteristics also link Brand to the Devil. Like Lucifer, he wants to overthrow the existing order so that he can rule himself. His all-consuming desire for power is identical to that of Lucifer, who storms Heaven, is defeated, and is then cast down into the pits of Hell. Moreover, Brand, like Lucifer, is a rebel from his own kind. Finally, Brand, like Lucifer, takes on supernatural aspects. Caine, yet another brother, kills him with a silver-tipped arrow made especially for that purpose because he comes to believe that Brand is no longer like the rest of the family. Though he does not explain exactly what he means by his comment, the implication is that he has become evil. The power of silver over evil and the supernatural is well-known in folklore. Werewolves are commonly killed with silver bullets, for example, and silver has a similar affect on evil in the Amber novels. This is established early in the series when, in *The Guns of Avalon*, Ganelon explains to Corwin how the people who remained within the black circle of evil spreading through the kingdom of Amber stole and pillaged everything but objects made of silver.

The novels also contain material which helps to create an impression of active evil in an almost subliminal manner through the process of repetition. For example, one scene in *Nine Princes in Amber* is set in Avernus, the entrance to the underworld in Roman mythology, and there are many references in the novel to devils. Some are very general; others, like those of Corwin's consort, Lorraine in *The Guns of Avalon*, are very specific. She mentions, for instance, "the Horned One himself" and "the goat-man."

By contrast, elements of a prototypic grail quest are buried in the novels. Corwin is clearly filling the task of the hero—restoration. There is a "freeing of the waters" scene at the end of *The Guns of Avalon*. The evolved symbols of the grail quest are present in the form of the Tarot, admittedly adapted to the purposes of the novels, but nonetheless present. There is an adapted "Sword Dance" in the ritual of tracing the Pattern. There is a "Medicine Man" adaptation in Corwin himself. He both causes the land to be healed and in a scene at the outset of *The Guns of Avalon*, he saves the life of a wounded knight named Sir Lancelot du Lac. And, there is a "Perilous Chapel/Perilous Cemetery" adaptation, replete with the encounter of a "terrible storm," an encounter with a Dead Body, in the form of Oberon's funeral procession, and a threat by a Black Hand, when Dworkin, the mad dwarf and grandfather of the clan, reverts to an original monsterlike form. These grail elements, originally identified by Jessie Weston in *From Ritual to Romance*, are further supported by Arthurian references. Taken together, they clearly form a complex of images and symbols, which, along with that of the unicorn, establish the presence of good in the novels. Set against the cluster of Devil and evil images, they further establish the moral values for the series by creating an old-fashioned conflict between good and evil.

Yet another use that Zelazny finds for myth is to expand and deepen the significance of his themes. Particularly in his early work, there is an enormous emphasis on renewal, or restoration, and the growth that leads to it. His recurrent and more specific themes of immortality, greed, vanity, love, fertility, guilt, revenge, sacrifice, individualism, and power, are underscored by the broader and more significant theme of renewal. It comes in many forms and on several scales. There is renewal of the individual, found in the many examples of personality metamorphosis which occur in his work, but which is spelled out most specifically in the character of Carlton Davits in "The Doors of His Mouth, the Lamps of His Face." There is renewal of a planet and a people, as found in *This Immortal* and "A Rose for Ecclesiastes." There is renewal of a society and a culture, as found in *Lord of Light*, and there is renewal of the universe, as found in the Amber novels.

This pervasive concern is primarily supported by mythic elements. Two techniques in particular expand and emphasize the renewal theme: the identification of the protagonists with various "dying and reviving gods" and buried, or prototypic, grail quests. The most explicit example of Zelazny's adaptation of the "dying and reviving god" motif occurs in *This Immortal*. The source of this model, as mentioned earlier, is Frazer's *Golden Bough*. According to him, such mythological deities as " . . . Osirus, Tammuz, Adonis, and Attis . . . represented the yearly decay and revival of life, especially of vegetable life, which they [the people of Egypt and Western Asia] personified as a god who annually died and rose again from the dead. In name and detail the rites varied from place to place: in substance they were the same." In other words, the gods were anthropomorphic versions of what was universally witnessed in nature, the changing of the seasons.

In *This Immortal*, Zelazny first identifies his protagonist, Conrad, with several gods who fit the "dying and reviving god" model by allusion, and then he reinforces the association by adapting several elements from the prototypic myth to his story. For example, the "dying and reviving god" is typically killed by being ripped or torn apart. Death is violent and sudden. Adonis is mangled by a wild boar. Attis, in one version, is gored to death by a boar, and in another version, he unmans himself and bleeds to death. Osirus, after being drowned in a coffer which was soldered shut and thrown into the Nile, was retrieved and his body was cut into fourteen parts and strewn throughout the land by Seth. And at the instigation of Juno, who was jealous of him, the baby Dionysius was ambushed by Titans, who cut him limb from limb, boiled the body with herbs, and then ate it. But while Zelazny cannot legitimately kill off Conrad because of the constraints which he has created in the world of the novel—Conrad's immortality, for instance—he does the next best thing. He kills off the identity. Karaghiosis is supposedly blown apart in the explosion of his blazeboat, and shortly thereafter, Conrad Nomikos appears. Figuratively, the god has died and been reborn.

Another element that Zelazny adapts from the model is the

connection of the "dying and reviving god" to the underworld. In a naive mind, it was logical to assume that when the vegetation disappeared in the late fall, its anthropomorphic equivalent had gone underground, especially when the plants reappeared the following spring from beneath the earth. By extension and recurrence, it was also logical to assume that the god was, in fact, Lord of the Underground. Such connections do exist for Tammuz, Adonis, and Hyacinth, who, according to Erwin Rhode, was probably "an old aboriginal deity of the underworld who had been worshipped at Amyclae long before the Dorians invaded and conquered the country." Both Dionysius and Osirus were recognized as connected to the underground simply through their respective titles of "Lord of the Underworld" and "Ruler of the Dead." It is thus easy to understand why Zelazny has taken such care to identify Conrad with the underworld, both symbolically and by allusion to the "dying and reviving gods." He too is a caretaker, the caretaker of an Earth that more closely resembles Hell than anything else because of its radiation and mutations.

Other elements from the various "dying and reviving god" myths are also adapted for the novel. For example, Conrad plays the syrinx for the satyrs; both Attis and Marsyas were pipers. The novel begins in October, which is the period commonly believed to have been the time when the ancient Greeks held their harvest festival. Conrad is Greek, and the harvest festival was held in celebration of the autumn seed-sowing. Conrad's sanctuary is the island of Cos, an island made famous by the poet Theocritis in his description of a festival to offer first fruits to Demeter from the barley stores, which the farmers believed she was responsible for. Finally, and most obviously, by the end of the novel Conrad's very presence promises the restoration of fertility to the land just as the reappearance of the reviving god does. In her investigations of the grail myths, Jessie Weston found that the restoration of fertility to the land was directly connected to the healing of the wounded king. So, it is no accident that the fortunes of Earth do not begin to brighten until after Conrad is cured of his fungus infection by the radioactivity of a "hot" rock.

The other device that Zelazny frequently uses to support the renewal theme is the buried grail myth. Such a prototypic myth has already been identified in the Amber novels, and grail myth elements are present in "A Rose for Ecclesiastes" as well as many of Zelazny's other stories.

While his manipulation of mythic elements is not always completely successful, it is always daring, inventive, and imaginative. Though it may not have been fully intended, Zelazny could not have picked a better field to experiment in than myth, for regardless of the exotic worlds he creates for his stories, they ultimately make a basic statement about man's daily experiences. And myth, if we are to believe Mark Schorer, is the instrument "by which we continually struggle to make our experiences intelligible to ourselves. A myth is a large, controlling image that gives philosophical meaning to the facts of ordinary life; that is, which has organizing value for experience." Further, it is "fundamental, the dramatic representation of our deepest instinctual life, of a primary awareness of man in the universe, capable of many configurations, upon which all particular opinions and attitudes depend."

In Zelazny's stories, the protagonists are usually sent upon psychological quests which parallel their physical ones. They quest for a balance in their personalities that will free them from their neuroses and elevate them to a new level of maturity. Under the whip of their experiences, Zelazny's protagonists achieve a growth of personality so enormous that it may be termed metamorphic. The new man is but a shadow of the former. Because the quests are usually realized, they support the renewal theme. Myth, as Zelazny uses it in most of his stories, helps to create the impression of psychological growth and deepens the significance of the personality metamorphosis when it finally occurs.

Once, when I asked Zelazny why he added a Noh play to "Damnation Alley" when he expanded it to novel length, he wrote:

> . . . I somewhat subscribe to the notion of a resonance-effect in literature. I think that if someone has had even a brief exposure to a particular medium, something that later mimes it will strike a chord of familiarity, even if he does not know why, even if, say, his only exposure to Noh was forgotten background sequences in *Sayonara*. A sense of familiarity is always a good thing to stir in a reader, as I see it, perhaps especially when he doesn't know

why. It makes a thing seem somehow more important if it nags him a bit.

This impulse to stir the reader is at work in Zelazny's experiments with mythic elements. It is the same generative impulse that makes the writer want to create, want to test himself, want to become the god of creative fire. And the result is, in Zelazny's case, quite literally fabulous.

7

Peter S. Alterman

FOUR VOICES IN ROBERT SILVERBERG'S DYING INSIDE

The power of language is astonishing. By judiciously selecting the right mix of words and stringing them together just so, a writer can create the whole universe within the mind of a reader. If, among the improbabilities the writer chooses, there are huge orbital space stations spinning against the blackness of interstellar space, or giant amoebae casually snacking on leg of starlet, well, then, we recognize the improbable reality created as science fiction. On the other hand, when the improbabilities are few—the landscape well known, the situations and characters drawn from everyday life—then they constitute mere fiction.

Like every other generalization about language, literature, and psychology, what I have just said won't really stand up to harsh analysis. Generally, however, it is fair to say that science fiction is more improbable than the novel of romantic intrigue. On the face of it, distinguishing science fiction from so-called realistic fiction would appear to be a fairly simple thing. After all, science fiction is demonstrably more improbable than fiction about current society, isn't it?

This question artfully leads to Robert Silverberg's novel *Dying Inside*, a science fiction novel whose protagonist is a genre cliché, a telepath. It is also a novel about the change in a man's life caused by aging, set in the real New York City of the early seventies. We could call this a novel about a man's "midlife crisis." No worlds are shattered, no galactic civilizations are

saved from conquest, not even one diabolical Russian spy plot
is discovered.

What does happen is that David Selig, the telepathic protagonist, loses his telepathic power (hence the title), is mugged by
black students on the steps of Columbia University's Low Library, and comes to a tentative rapprochement with his sister.
During the course of the novel, we learn about David's past, his
worries, thoughts, and private ecstasies; we discover the interior
life of a telepath. Through flashbacks we learn the effects of
telepathy on David's childhood, his emotional relationships, the
two women he had lived with, the only other telepath he has
ever known, and above all, his sister. It doesn't sound much like
science fiction, does it?

But *Dying Inside* is generally considered science fiction, and
very good science fiction at that. Also, it's not as though the novel
of character hasn't been successfully written as science fiction.
Frederik Pohl did it in *Gateway*; Delany's *Triton* did it in a
completely different way. Olaf Stapledon's *Sirius* and *Odd John*
come to mind also.

The real distinction between *Dying Inside* and the formula
telepath stories is scope. The scope of *Dying Inside* is the private,
psychological life of one inconspicuous man doing nothing more
sinister than ghostwriting student papers for hire, but who is
losing the single most basic part of his identity, his gift for reading
minds. This focus has been called, disparagingly, the curse of
Henry James. *Dying Inside* is an example of how unfair that
generalization can be. A novel which can create a realistic picture
of the psychological life of a telepath can reveal things about
telepathy which all the suspense and adventure fiction in the
genre cannot. For one, it can tell us what it's like to read minds,
and how it feels to do it.

Dying Inside is also about dying and being reborn. In 1971
and 1972, when this novel was written, Silverberg also published
a number of other works concerned with death and rebirth.
Among them are *Downward to the Earth*, a novel about a former
colonial administrator's search for rebirth on the alien world he
once managed; *Son of Man*, a strange novel in which the human
protagonist meets a series of characters who are future human
forms; *The Second Trip*, about a man who returns to society after

the equivalent of a personality transplant; and the novella "Born
With the Dead," in which the protagonist follows his beloved
wife through death and revivification. Clearly, the themes of
death and rebirth were churning around inside Silverberg's head
during the time *Dying Inside* was written.

Dying Inside is a tapestry woven from flashbacks, contemporary narrative, excerpts from essays, and confessions. The
flashbacks show what telepathy meant to David's earlier life and
identity. The essays he writes show his grasp of expository prose,
his intellectual competence (the papers are too good to be stu-
dent-written), and are used incidentally to comment on his personal situation. In the contemporary narrative, David Selig's
story is of a ghostwriter who is beaten by a dissatisfied customer.
Along the way he memorializes the death of his power to read
minds, has dinner with his sister, attends a faculty party, and has
dinner with his sister a second time.

When we are introduced to David in chapter one, we immediately learn about his literary ability and how he makes his
living. In this chapter alone he quotes Eliot twice, Beckett once,
and cites Yeats. During the course of the novel, his grasp of
Western humanities becomes evident. He is at home with Kafka's
novels, ancient Greek poetry and drama, Montaigne, Virgil, and
Dante. He quotes Huxley, Wiener, and the Curé d'Ars. He's
somewhat pompous—imagine, "Poor goofy Yeats"! David is obsessed by his age. Writing about Kafka's novels, he says:

> The two books represent varying attempts at telling the same
> story, that of the existentially disengaged man who is suddenly
> involved in a situation from which there is no escape, and who,
> after making attempts to achieve the grace that will release him
> from his predicament, succumbs.

This is an excellent summary of David's own condition and of
the course of the novel.

The goal Kafka's Joseph K reaches for is the goal David strives
for: grace in acceptance of the inevitable. His power is dying,
the power which has both blighted and illuminated his life:

> It's always been a curse to him, hasn't it? It's cut him off from his
> fellow men and doomed him to a loveless life. . . . On the other
> hand, without the power, what are you? Without that one faltering

unpredictable unsatisfactory means of contact with them, how will you be able to touch them at all? . . . You love it and you despise it, this gift of yours. You dread losing it despite all it's done to you. You'll fight to cling to the last shreds of it, even though you know the struggle's hopeless.

The last line here emphasizes David's identification with Joseph K.

David's soul is cleft; he loathes his ability and at the same time he clings to it. On the novel's first page, he splits himself in two. He speaks of "myself and . . . that creature which lives within me, skulking in its spongy lair and spying on unsuspecting mortals." David rejects his power; he distances himself from it psychically. It is the fault of his telepathy that David is isolated, unloved, a failure.

His power has condemned him to being "society's ugliest toad, the eavesdropper, the voyeur." He is Leopold Bloom of *Ulysses* watching his wife tupped by Blazes Boylan, through a keyhole. The connection between telepathic power and sexual potency is emphasized throughout *Dying Inside*. David's sister frequently refers to the connection, and David makes much of it himself. When David finally admits his secret to his sister Judith, it is in the context of his knowing about her sex life. The words she uses in responding to his revelation are touchstones of the telepathy-sexuality connection: " . . . why I always felt dirty when I was a kid and you were around. . . . If I ever catch you poking around in my head after this, I'll cut your balls off."

That David equates his telepathic power with sexual power is not pathological, though. Athletes equate their sexual potency with their special prowess, as do many writers. This is a nice bit of psychological realism: telepathy *feels* like any other ability; it's part of one's identity, and therefore part of one's sexual identity. This particular conjunction, however, is poisoned. Since David cannot send his thoughts, but only receive, he sees himself as passive, a voyeur. The problem with the power is transferred, psychologically, to the personality.

As a voyeur, David feels isolated. The only other telepath he meets, Tom Nyquist, is aghast at this attitude:

"The problem is that I feel isolated from other human beings."
"Isolated? You? . . . How can you pretend you're isolated?"

> "The information I get is useless," Selig said. "I can't act on
> it. I might just as well not be reading it in."

This is the heart of the irony. David can watch, but not act. His
telepathic power gives him access to a keyhole; it is not a key.

David feels isolated by his telepathic power because it is essentially passive. Nonetheless, it is a form of communication.
Without it, David is alone; his one method of communicating
with the world is gone. This argument seems to be quite reasonable, except that telepathy has kept him isolated. Release
from telepathy—to be merely normal—should imply revivification. After all, he no longer will be part of the .001% of humanity with the power to read minds. He won't be a voyeur
anymore.

But no. David dreads the death of his power as a descent into
absolute isolation. Without his telepathy, who is he? "Where's
my identity? I'm Selig the Mindreader, right? The Amazing
Mental Man. So if I stop being him—" One of the things David
is, without his power, is normal, mortal. Look back to the above
quotation from page one of the novel and note the word "mortals." There's a key to his desire to keep his power: it makes him
godlike. He thinks of himself as more than mortal, and when his
power dies, it leaves "behind this merely mortal husk of mine."

The connection between godhood and telepathy is another
true note this novel chimes, like the association between potency
and telepathy. David thinks of himself as a Christ. He parodies
Jesus' words, as in "let nothing human be alien to me" and he
fears crucifixion if his ability is ever discovered: "They'd all love
me. Loving me, they'd beat me to a pulp."

The twin themes of communion and godhood join together in
the ecstasy which the telepathy provides him, and transcendence
is the watchword.

> Yes! Oh, the joining, the touching, the union, the oneness! No
> longer is he David Selig. He is a part of them, and they are a part
> of him, and in that joyous blending he experiences loss of self, he
> gives up all that is tired and worn and sour in him, he gives up
> his fears and uncertainties, he gives up everything that has sep-
> arated himself from himself for so many years. He breaks through.
> He is fully open and the immense signal of the universe rushes

freely into him. He receives. He transmits. He absorbs. He radiates. Yes. Yes. Yes. Yes.

In his transcendent state he is not David Selig. He is all. The union is sexual, godlike, total. It surpasses the receive-only condition of his power. Actually, it is mystical. The acquiescence of the four "yesses" at the end of the quote above is practically orgasmic. It is also the state of grace he aspires to as his power dies.

This condition of ecstasy is the one true gift David has gleaned from his telepathic power—an orgasm of selflessness, the joy of losing one's ego in something larger than oneself. In these ecstatic moments of total contact, David mines "the real stuff, the whole person." At bottom, David's transcendental ecstasy is a way of getting outside himself, of being part of someone or something else. Without it, he is caught inside himself, which one would think would be a fate David would desire. After all, in the privacy of his own mind he can be himself. And yet, that circumstance is just one which frightens him, because it is one he has never experienced. The privacy and silence terrify him. They trap him inside his single self and he is permanently cut off from the ecstasy he has known.

David equates the coming silence with death. In an interior essay written in the term paper style, David links communication and entropy to death:

> Human beings, says Wiener, carry on anti-entropic processes. We have sensory receptors. We communicate with one another. We make use of what we learn from one another. . . . But what if a human being *turns* himself, inadvertantly or by choice, into an isolated system? . . . Gradually the chaos expands in him, gradually the forces of entropy seize possession of this ganglion, that synapse. He takes in a decreasing amount of sensory data until his surrender to entropy is complete. . . . This condition is known as death.

So not only is David's loss of telepathy a reverse apotheosis, a loss of potency, a loss of identity and isolation from the living, it is death. Personal death as well as the "heat-death of the universe."

In fact, looking at the language of these citations, it would appear that David equates his condition (aging) with the process of universal entropic decay. At the beginning of the novel, David compares himself to Prufrock, Malone and Bloom. Here he compares himself to the universe.

And why not? The transcendental ecstasy of David's telepathic communions does make him part of a larger whole. It is, however, true that the whole is indifferent to the fate of one of its motes. This is why the correspondence between David and the universe is weak, and an example of the exaggerations of self-pity which he is heir to throughout the novel.

Structurally, the novel presents us with a correspondence between the decay of David's telepathic power and the decay of Western civilization. Not only does David's ability to read minds knit him into society more intensely than normal, but he is a fount of Western humanism. He lives by it for the purposes of his papers, and because of his mastery of the subjects coupled with his telepathic ability to read his clients' minds, he can always deliver and guarantee his work.

Except for Yahya Lumumba. David has difficulty with Lumumba's paper because he cannot find an appropriate voice to use. He dips into Lumumba's mind and finds it "A roaring furnace . . . I can't handle this volcanic blast." Not only is David driven off by the intensity of the mind, his power actually shuts down: "Never have I lost my grip and slipped from a mind like this. I look up, dazed, shattered." This last quote highlights the connection between Lumumba's hatred and David's coming psychic impotence, as Lumumba beats David unconscious, following which David loses his power for good.

Besides the obvious hatred Lumumba has, the second and more significant reason that David cannot produce the paper is that Lumumba has no ties to Western culture:

> . . . *Europydes Sophocles Eeskilus why the fuck do I have to know anything about them to write anything about them what good is it to a black man those old dead Greek fuckers how are they relevant to the black experience relevant relevant relevant . . .*

Not only is Lumumba unable to write the essay, he cannot find a reference point in his experience for it.

In effect, David fails to satisfy Lumumba with a paper because Lumumba's young life, both in and out of the university, is an artifact of society's sports culture. David, of course, is unconcerned with trivialities such as college basketball. Yet to Lumumba, basketball is truly the only important issue in his life. It got him into college, presumably. Writing papers on Greek plays did not. The black youth (the future) is divorced from the cultural tradition of Western civilization (*Europydes Sophocles Eeskilus*). Furthermore, Lumumba hates the purveyors of such knowledge (David, the assignment, Jews). David's other jock clients at least find their cultural inheritance relevant, if not accessible. Symbolically, hatred, violence, and physical activity, supersede the more genteel and intellectual characteristics of the old society.

It is pretty clear that David is losing a lot, but as we have come to expect in this novel, there is a more mundane side to the issue. David bemoans not only the loss of his power, but his loss of hair, the death of his contemporaries, and the rise to power of those younger than he. The death of his power is just a warmup for the real thing. Since he cannot reverse time, entropy, or the loss of his telepathic power, David must accept inevitability; he tries to be a good Joseph K. This he does by groping his way unsteadily towards a bond with his sister Judith.

At the outset of the novel, Judith is attempting to reconcile herself with David after years of hostility. David is not a willing partner to the reconciliation at first: "Her love is unpalatable to me, and her sentimentalism is even less to my taste. . . . Her remorse for her past coldness toward me has a flavor even more stinking than her newfound love." He feels this way partly because he still mistrusts her for "all the years when she treated me like a circus attraction" and consequently his perception of their relationship is dark:

> We're locked in a kind of marriage, Judith and I, an old burned-out marriage held together with skewers.

As David loses his ability to read minds, he finds himself drawn increasingly to her. She is the only person he can discuss his condition with, for one thing. For another, she is his only living relative, his only source of love, no matter how bitter. She confides her sexual and romantic concerns to him, in return for his love.

When David recounts the story of his revealing his power to her, he discovers the kernel of closeness hidden within him: she never used the knowledge of his telepathy against him. It is as if recognizing this allows David to draw closer to her, and as an example, he attends a party given by one of her lovers at her request. At the end of the novel, when he is merely human, David accepts and returns her love: "I embrace her warmly, pulling her tight against my body for perhaps a minute."

David is learning that he can communicate; that his loss can actually be seen as a gain, and that love can become a distinct possibility in his life. His growing love for Judith is the touchstone of the change, of course, but he projects that potential onto a fantasized meeting with ex-lover Toni, and into an imaginary letter to his lost love, Kitty:

> As the power slips away from me, as it dies, perhaps there's a chance for an ordinary human relationship between us at last, of the kind that ordinary human beings have all the time.

David sees the potential for a normal life in the vacuum left behind by his vanishing telepathic power, and he acts on it. *Dying Inside* ends with the family, or marriage, as David points out, reunited, held together by mutual caring rather than by skewers. The feel of it is reminiscent of the happy endings of Shakespeare's comedies, where marriages not only restore order to the specific relationships, but to the State and to Nature as well.

David is a mortal at the end of the novel, one who can give and receive love. He still is not secure in his identity, still shocked and filled with loss. But he has touched grace, and he feels that acceptance is within reach. The novel ends with David saying "hello" four times, echoing the accepting "yes" of his last telepathic moments.

David's acceptance and achievement of grace are important to the novel because they come only after he acknowledges that he does want to keep his ability, which is an important developmental step. The method he attempts to use to reclaim his dying power (a feat he acknowledges to be impossible) appears in the fifth chapter, which is an essaylike discussion of Huxley's theory of a "cerebral reducing valve" which filters out paranormal insights, thus allowing daily life to be lived. From this conceit, David proceeds to speculate on the physiology of self-abuse as a means of opening the reducing valve. Since he wants to revivify his power, flagellation seems like a possible tactic. So for the rest of the novel David flays himself with emotionally painful recollections.

It doesn't work, of course, as he knew it wouldn't. Yet by knowing that he is doomed (a fact he repeats often), he gains one distinct advantage. It assures him that he will be a tragic figure like Joseph K and reach a form of grace, rather than K., "who simply sinks lower and lower . . . so crushed by the general tragedy of the times that he is incapable of any tragedy on an individual level. K. is a pathetic figure, Joseph K a tragic one." Knowing he is doomed and that he can only accept assures David that he is not K., who could not even reach that perception.

Within the mundane world of David's 1976 New York, the grandeur of this goal transforms itself into skipping a Chinese dinner. David isn't only mocking himself in that, though. He's also truly ambivalent and unable to believe in the restoration of his power. Beside that, the rest of chapter six, from which the Chinese dinner transformation is taken, is pretty unusual.

For one thing, it's only a single short paragraph long. For another, the paragraph begins in the third person: "But why does David Selig want his power to come back?", slides into the second person: "On the other hand, without the power, what are you?", and finishes in the first person: "I'll skip the chow mein." It's as much as he can do in his world, skipping a meal; at least it is an acknowledgment of his desire to keep the power.

Now, recognizing the strangeness of chapter six, think about the "essays" in chapters four, fourteen, and twenty-three, and the fact that chapters two, twelve, sixteen, twenty, twenty-two and twenty-five are written in the third person.

Most of these latter are flashbacks, separated in time from David's present. Moreover, they are all focused on the experience of being telepathic. Chapter two is an interview David has with a school psychologist which clarifies how then-current behavioral sciences failed to deal with either David's telepathy or anxiety. Chapter twelve exemplifies the experience of David's telepathic ecstasies. In chapter sixteen, David meets Tom Nyquist, another telepath, and we understand how two telepaths communicate. Chapter twenty is another childhood flashback, to a time when David's power was almost discovered in school. Chapter twenty-two documents David's meeting Kitty Holstein and his inability to read her mind. In chapter twenty-five, David finally loses his telepathic power and his former way of life.

To see how important the question of voice is to the novel, look back at the very first paragraph of the first chapter of the novel. Near the end of the paragraph, the following appears:

> Let us go then, you and I, when the morning is spread out against the sky. . . .
> You and I. To whom do I refer? I'm heading downtown alone, after all. *You and I.*
> Why, of course I refer to myself and to that creature which lives within me, skulking in its spongy lair . . .

The "you and I" are introduced as part of the reference to Eliot's "Prufrock," but quickly David picks up the words and focuses on them.

You and I. David is a man split in two. He sees himself as separated into David Selig and the power of telepathy. This division strengthens our sense of how divided he is on the question of his telepathy. It also is an intimate device for speaking directly to the reader. For example, looking back on chapter six, the "you" clearly refers to himself. Yet at the end of chapter nineteen the "you" referred to is clearly the reader:

> What the hell are you doing reading someone else's mail? Don't you have any decency? I can't show you this.

In this section, we are put into the role of voyeur which David accuses himself of, and then treated accordingly. The whole chapter has this sense of direct communication between David and the reading audience. The tour of his life furnishings isn't for his own benefit so much as it is for ours.

Although there is one point of view in *Dying Inside*, there are four voices: "I," "you," "he," and none. Each, in its own way, contributes to enlarging the reality of David's telepathy. The sections of the novel written from the "I" are immediate in time and impact. We have immediate access to David's thoughts and feelings in these sections, as well as his actions. We are embedded in David's mind just as he can imbed himself in other minds. The process works as a mirror.

In the sections written in the "you" voice, David is either talking to his split self, a technique which dramatizes the duality he believes in, or directly to the reader. Either way, the communication is less intimate than the unobtrusive intimacy of the implied listener of the "I" sections. When David is talking to "you," he is more self-conscious. An example of this is his retreat from exposure in the quote from chapter nineteen, above. When his "I" writes an imaginary letter to Kitty, the pain David feels is obvious. He abruptly becomes aware of his audience, though, and shuts the letter off. He increases the distance; he guards his privacy.

The chapters written in the "he" voice are more distant yet. They are flashbacks in his personal history, and as such they are about David Seligs who are no longer the David Selig who is losing his telepathic power. They are in the past, which is distance. They are also about the experience of being telepathic. In this novel, it is imperative that we experience what it feels like to be telepathic. The focus on the telepathic experience nicely couples with the distance that using "he" creates, for it shows David isolating himself from the telepathic David (the "you" of page one). And, since this is David's special experience, use of the "he" distances the reader further in a way which adds stylistic impact to David's claim that his power isolates him from the rest of humanity.

And then there are two apparently nontelepathic chapters, twenty-two and twenty-five, written in the third person. In chapter twenty-two, David meets Kitty and finds that he cannot read her mind. Here the distance from self which the "he" provides is a good match for the isolation David feels from the woman he loves. In chapter twenty-five, David wakes in a hospital after having been beaten unconscious. Then, before the Dean of Columbia, he experiences a transcendental moment of ecstasy, and his power dies.

First, the distance of the "he" construction is a stylistic match for the alienation of the hospital, where he is first ignored, then treated impersonally. The fact that, in the former chapter, he cannot read Kitty's mind is an obvious parallel construction. Second, the transcendent ecstasy belongs to the list of telepathic experiences described in the third person in earlier chapters. Third, David's loss, finally, of his power is a profoundly isolating experience, and being far from his perspective reinforces that fact. The style matches the content and reinforces it.

The three "essays" which dot the novel are papers that David writes, two for students, one to himself. In each, the subject ostensibly is an intellectual analysis of a nonpersonal issue: Kafka's novels, the Oresteian myth cycle, and information theory, entropy, and death. And yet, each comments directly on David's condition. Joseph K's problem is David's problem. The truncated discussion of the "Electra theme" is about interpreting an act from several different perspectives. This we do with the different "voices." It is also the beginning of a discussion about the interaction of the individual and destiny, another of David's concerns.

Finally, David's essay on communication, entropy, and death ties the essay from explicitly into an analysis of his condition. In a paper on "Entropy as a Factor in Everyday Life," for "Selig Studies" run by "Prof. Selig," he discusses his perception of the relationship between lack of communication and death, a highly emotional topic for him.

These dispassionate essays offer relevant parallels to the larger concerns of David's stories. They are overviews, though, theories, like Huxley's "cerebral reducing valve," which define the larger structure—the philosophical underpinnings—of David's loss. They help answer the question of why we should care about David and his problems. He is not just a freak, he is a man who is living through an experience which, in many ways, is fundamental to us all. The stylistic sleight-of-hand is designed to offer us a share of that experience.

The four different voices of *Dying Inside* allow Silverberg to alter the focal distance between us and David. From deep within his mind, we can pull back to look at the larger picture, the philosophical implications and the story of David's loss of his telepathic power. The skill with which the style enhances the themes help knit them smoothly into a very believable story about a very believable man. The "Amazing Mental Man" comes alive in *Dying Inside*.

Patrick L. McGuire

FUTURE HISTORY, SOVIET STYLE: The Work of the Strugatsky Brothers

In the late 1950s, after near-total suppression during the Stalin years, Soviet science fiction began to rebuild. As was practically inevitable, this reconstruction involved extensive borrowing from English-language SF, especially the American, which had assumed the world lead in the genre during the years when the Soviet field was moving toward extinction. Among the new importations from America was the "future history"—the practice of setting a number of more or less independent stories within a common background of posited historical events and scientific discoveries, possibly with some continuing characters or at least allusions to them. Ivan Efremov, who had opened up the modern era of Soviet science fiction with his sweeping *Andromeda* in 1957, also helped to introduce the future history. Two additional works, the polemical novelette "Cor Serpentis" (1959) and the antiutopia *The Hour of the Bull* (1969; untranslated), are set at intervals of several centuries in the same future history as *Andromeda*. Efremov, however, resorted to large chunks of lecturing to present background material. He never mastered the feel of a "lived-in" future, a concept that first brought fame to Robert Heinlein and then became a standard tool of American science fiction writers. The first Soviet writers to attain this were the collaborating brothers Arkady and Boris Strugatsky. Most, though not all, of their straight science fiction (they have also written satire and absurdist fantasy) fits together into a single future history which so far includes at least ten works of book or near-book length and covers the period from the late twentieth century to the late twenty-third.

While vivid and fairly detailed, in most respects the Strugatsky future history is not too surprising to the Western reader. The majority of its elements find parallels in the future histories of, say, Heinlein, Niven, or Le Guin. But some of its features are uniquely Soviet. Of these, some are a result of Russian historical experience, while others derive from the program adopted at the Twenty-Second Party Congress (1961), and from other guidelines and prohibitions issued by the regime's ideological watchdogs (including editors and critics, as well as censors per se). The single greatest demand upon the Soviet SF writer—and not too unreasonable a one, granted the premise that Marxism-Leninism is a "science"—is that every story should reflect the teachings of Marxism-Leninism on the nature of societies in general and on the future course of history in our society in particular. This requirement has a number of applications. For one thing, Marxism-Leninism predicts that the "socialist camp" led by the Soviet Union will spread to encompass the whole world and will then develop into full communism, characterized by the motto "from each according to his ability, to each according to his need." Consequently, this entails the attainment of "material abundance," the abolition of money, the withering away of the state, and other features described in the writings of Marx and his followers. The transition to world socialism may be violent or fairly peaceful; the capitalist ruling circles may see the handwriting on the wall and consent to the inevitable, and for their part the socialists may simply buy the capitalists off to prevent bloodshed. At least in science fiction, the date for the transition is usually set at between 2000 and 2050.

What is more, since the triumph of communism derives from universally valid "scientific" laws, it is to be expected that any starfaring extraterrestrials will similarly have left capitalism and violence behind them; there can be no Soviet *Star Wars*. Similarly, within each society, crime and most other causes of strife will all but disappear and hence are not available to the writer for dramatic conflict. Other familiar science fictional devices, including time travel, "alternate worlds," social retrogression on a "lost colony" or after a war, and the depiction of nuclear war on Earth are either forbidden outright or are hedged with restrictions. It is within these boundaries set by the regime that the Strugatskys have been obliged to erect their fictional framework. Still, it is not much of a constraint to be forbidden to do what you do not want to do in any case. The Strugatsky brothers certainly are neither neo-Stalinists on the one hand nor traditionalist ethnic-Russian nationalists on the other, but their true views might lie almost anywhere on the spectrum of Soviet thought between these points. It is entirely possible that they are, and more particularly, were when they started writing, exactly what they present themselves as—mildly liberal Marxist-Leninists.

In early Strugatsky stories, much of the drama emerges from the strife of man against nature. "Night on Mars" (1960, included in *Noon, 22nd Century*) seems to be set in the later 1970s or early 1980s, and is thus the first story by internal chronology. It describes the trek of two doctors who must fight off the notorious Martian flying leeches to attend the woman giving birth to the first baby on Mars. *Land of the Crimson Clouds* (1959, untranslated) was the Strugatskys' first novel and remains one of their longest works—the brothers incline toward novella or short novel length, relying on their future history as a whole or on more particular linkages between works to provide a feeling of scope. *Land* describes an expedition to the stormy deserts of Venus to open up for exploitation a uranium deposit that had been discovered from orbit. The novel is set probably in the late 1980s, and it introduces the first continuing set of Strugatsky heroes, chief among them stolid Anton Bykov and excitable Vladimir Yurkovsky. Ten years later in "Destination: Amalthea" (1960) the same group, augmented by Ivan Zhilin, an engineer fresh out of the space academy, sets off on a rescue mission to a scientific station on a moon of Jupiter, only to find themselves stranded on a spaceship floating like a balloon in the dense Jovan atmosphere.

Along with the struggle against nature, the interplay of personalities (chiefly the brave but painstaking Bykov versus the brilliant but impulsive Yurkovsky) provides movement. In works of this period the Strugatskys pay much attention to hard science and technology. Their treatments of the environments on Mars and Venus are indeed a trifle optimistic even by the standards of the time, but essentially accurate (though now of course totally obsolete); their depiction of Jupiter would need only minor revision even today. The brothers lovingly detail the progression from atomic-powered spaceships carrying reaction mass to more advanced "photon ships" and then on to interstellar ships powered by Bussard engines ("ramscoops"). Indeed, the Strugatskys made several references to ramscoops in stories published in 1960, the very same year that the American Robert Bussard first proposed the concept. Social developments are not ignored, though they are mentioned only in passing. The USSR has already drawn even with the West economically, but the capitalists seem to be going to their historical doom quite meekly. At least a partial disarmament is in effect by the 1980s (Bykov is a graduate of the Surface Transport School, "the former Armor School"), and extensive international cooperation is the rule in space. Ships are manned chiefly by citizens of one country (though in the Soviet case, the Strugatskys are careful to give representation to non-Russian nationalities; Bykov's companion Dauge is a Latvian), but they cooperate and they may have foreign guests aboard. Even more striking, and frequently lost in the translation, is the internationalism exhibited in the Strugatskys' word coinages. The "crawler" in "Night on Mars" is just that, a *krauler* borrowed from English-language SF. The slang term for Jupiter is "Jupe" (*Dzhup*), from the English rather than the Russian *Iupiter*. The Strugatskys are also fond of dropping bits of English, French, German, Japanese, and (in early works) Chinese into their dialog. Whether it results from censorship guidelines or not, this peaceful, internationalist approach stands in striking contrast to Western science fiction of the late fifties and early sixties, which frequently took World War III as part of the background even when a given story did not belong to the legion of overt after-the-bomb works.

The next two stories by internal chronology continue the theme of space adventure, but begin to shift the emphasis from technology to individual psychology and to social developments. "Almost the Same" (1960, included in *Noon: 22nd Century*) is set in about 2002 in the Advanced School of Cosmonautics, the same academy from which Zhilin had graduated. The story strongly recalls, and may have been inspired by, parts of Heinlein's *Space Cadet*, but the Strugatsky work is both shorter in length and closer to us in time. Indeed, while there is talk of photon ships and ramscoops offstage, the depicted astronaut training equipment was in many aspects already obsolete by American standards of the 1960s. In any case, the story concentrates chiefly on questions of self-doubt, resoluteness, and final achievement which are, at least in English, traditional to the service academy story whether in or out of science fiction. "Almost the Same" also serves to introduce to us fledgling cosmonaut Sergei Kondratev, who will figure in later works. Social developments in the world outside the academy are treated only obliquely, but the Strugatskys do provide fictional support for Khrushchev's largely unrealized plan to require a year of work experience before admission to higher education, and they mention that an American or British company, "United Rocket Construction" (in English in the original) has just been nationalized—another victory for creeping socialism.

The second story of this grouping, *Space Apprentice* (1962), is once again about a sort of education, but here the Strugatskys have set themselves the more difficult task of depicting the emerging new communist personality as embodied in the young hero of the book, vacuum-welder Yura Borodin. Yura, the only blue-collar worker to star in any Strugatsky work (he probably owes his occupation to another Khrushchevian campaign of the period), is trying to get to Rhea, a moon of Saturn, to rejoin his workmates on a construction project. He hitches a ride with Yurkovsky, who by now is an inspector-general for the International Administration of Cosmic Communications, Bykov, and companions. It is now about 2007, and these adventurers are getting on in years, into their mid-fifties. Even Zhilin is now about thirty-three; he has been in space for a decade and is beginning to ask himself about the point of it all. As these veterans journey to various planets, moons, asteroids, and space stations along Yurkovsky's inspection route, they attempt to impart to young Borodin some of their experience of life.

Here too we can see a parallel with Heinlein—the education

of the young and naive by the old and wise is perhaps this author's most common theme. A difference in the Strugatsky view is that the old, while they have much to teach, are not infallible—for instance, near the end of the book Yurkovsky dies while taking an imprudent risk—and that the goal is not to replicate the previous generation, to produce a new crop of Heinlein Individuals, but rather to produce the new sort of personality which will be in harmony with the social stage of full communism. The chief obstacle the Strugatskys see on the road to this goal is *meshchanstvo*, a concept usually but somewhat inaccurately translated as "philistinism." A philistine is someone narrowly and smugly conventional, especially about art and culture. A *meshchanin* is someone more generally selfish and petty-minded, unable to see even his own long-term advantage. In the Strugatsky view, *meshchanstvo* is the guiding principle of advanced capitalist society, a spiritual malaise that persists even when many of capitalism's material difficulties have been resolved. In the socialist world, *meshchanstvo* is a survival from the past rather than an inherent vice, but it lingers on. Capitalist *meshchanstvo* is represented in *Space Apprentice* by the crime that Westerners import to a Central Asian international spaceport, by the narrow money-grubbing worldview of a Western cafe-owner concessionaire there, and, in space, by a corrupt asteroid-mining operation. The milder socialist strain is exemplified by Yurkovsky's sister (Dauge's ex-wife), who finds no purpose to her existence now that the social necessity for toil and sacrifice is gone, and by Shershen, the director of a Soviet space observatory, who has been playing his subordinates off one against the other and getting himself listed as coauthor of all their research publications.

In *Space Apprentice*, after Yurkovsky's death and the experience of teaching Yura Borodin, Zhilin decides that the real work of the future lies in education, and accordingly, that he will retire from space and return to Earth. We next meet him a little over a decade later, in about 2019, in *The Final Circle of Paradise* (1965). By this time he has changed professions once again, retiring from teaching and becoming a secret agent for the United Nations.

Noon: 22nd Century includes a brief news article dated 8 October 2021, announcing that an experimental spacecraft has been lost with all hands. Among the missing are Slavin (the baby born in "Night on Mars") and Kondratev (from "Almost the Same"). One very subtle touch in the article is a reference to the USCR instead of USSR. The implication is that by this date the Union of Soviet *Socialist* Republics has become the Union of Soviet *Communist* Republics: the Soviet Union has attained full communism. As for Slavin and Kondratev, their ship has (to use a handy cliché the authors avoid) hit a time warp, and it will soon reappear another century into the future, where the bulk of the stories in *Noon: 22nd Century* are set. Just before the cosmonauts' reappearance comes "The Conspirators" (1962), set in the same boarding school where Zhilin had been a teacher, but much later, in perhaps 2117.

Many Marxist theoreticians have predicted that under full communism, children will be raised communally in boarding schools while retaining ties to their parents. In the early sixties, Khrushchev tried to take the first steps toward realization of this concept, but he was soundly defeated on both economic and sentimental grounds. The idea of packing a young child off to a distant school has never attracted the Russians the way it has, say, the British elite. The Strugatskys, however, are genuinely attached to the boarding school concept, and they have continued to depict such schools in their work long after the official push for the idea has evaporated. "The Conspirators" exhibits the Strugatsky ideal for such a school: individualized computer-assisted instruction combined with loving attention from a professional, respected tutor who has only a few charges at a time. Fundamentally, the Strugatsky approach seems at least as much Platonic or Confucian as it does Marxist. Formal education, much more than the work experience or an alteration in the economic base of society, appears as the indispensible factor for the formation of the communist personality.

The plot of "The Conspirators" involves a romantic scheme to run away and join the newly announced terraforming project on Venus. The scheme, and the behavior of the young characters in general, indeed seems so immature that the editor of the English translation knocked two years off everyone's age, although this may reflect the much touted early sophistication of the

American adolescent rather than faulty observation by the
Strugatskys.

The children from "The Conspirators" reappear as adults in
later stories in and out of *Noon*, but first we come back to Slavin
and Kondratev, the returned space travellers who must now ac-
commodate themselves to the world of fully developed communism. Despite initial apprehensions, the cosmonauts find that
people are not radically different, just more considerate and pol-
ite, and on the average, better, with *meshchanstvo* all but erad-
icated. Technological advance has rendered the cosmonauts'
skills obsolete, so Slavin becomes a journalist and Kondratev, in
a move recalling Clarke's *The Deep Range*, joins the Oceanic
Guard, which, among other things, herds whales. The professions give us the opportunity to see many of the aspects of life
in the twenty-second century: the agricultural and industrial es-
tablishments by which want has been eliminated, and the scientific research into which an increasing portion of humankind's
effort is being invested. Both cosmonauts also find understanding
wives. One is Japanese and the other has an Irish-Hungarian
name, again illustrating the internationalization of the world.

By now exploration has pushed outward to the stars. The Strugatsky future history posits a new star catalog whose initials are
EN. Characters can then journey to EN 17, EN 101, or EN 2657
without obliging the authors to look up the type, mass, lumi-
nosity, etc., of Beta Hydrae or Wolf 294. However, at least for
some SF writers, such astronomical research provides useful intellectual discipline and may suggest story ideas. The adaptation
of this effort-saving device is symptomatic of a continued Strugatsky drift away from hard science and technology, though these
never disappear from the background of the authors' science
fictional works. One scheme for naming the planets of these stars
is to add "-a" to the name of its discoverer: Saula, Leonida,
Vladislava. The last of these, as it happens, is the scene of "The
Assaultmen." The story takes its name from the title of an organization specializing in scientific research in hazardous environments, but moving always with prudence—echoes of the
Yurkovsky-Bykov conflict. The story is less notable for its plot
than its commentary on the "Wanderers." As had been spelled

out in earlier stories, the Wanderers are an extraterrestrial race whose enigmatic archeological remains have been discovered on a number of worlds starting with Mars, a logical extension of a suggestion of the Soviet astronomer I. S. Shklovsky that the moons of Mars were artificial. The Pathfinder Corps, another paramilitary scientific organization, has been set up to study the remains of the Wanderers and other intelligent species. But not until "The Assaultmen" do we get a good look at a Wanderer artifact, and even then the stripped-down, abandoned space station orbiting Vladislava offers few clues about its makers. One of the chief functions served by extraterrestrials in the Strugatsky corpus is to evoke a sense of awe and mystery. To further this end, the aliens must be kept offstage as much as possible. "The Assaultmen" also introduces us to the trio of Leonid Gorbovsky, who had made earlier solo appearances, Mark Falkenstein, and Percy Dickson (or "Dixon," depending on the transliteration), who thereafter appear in many stories, playing the same role that Bykov, Yurkovsky, and companions had a century earlier. Also introduced here is the pompous, tactless, and marginally competent German, August Bader. The Strugatskys evidently see hidden virtues in him, since he recurs in later stories in ever-higher positions.

After centuries of searching and a number of indirect encounters, humanity finally makes a solid contact with extraterrestrial intelligence in the form of the natives of the planet Leonida in "The Planet with All the Conveniences." The Leonidan civilization is based on biology rather than physics, which both provides the basis of the plot—in its outlines, a standard one in the West—and perhaps explains why the Leonidans do not play much of a role in later stories. In the closing scene of *Noon*, Gorbovsky is about to depart on a contact mission to another newly discovered race, the Tagorans, but we learn nothing at all more about them for several books.

Once past *Noon: 22nd Century*, we encounter certain problems with the dating and relative order of stories. The author had arrived at a point in the future beyond the purview of the Party programs or any but the most general dicta of Marx or Lenin, while at the same time their own interests, and perhaps, opinions were shifting. Like most SF writers, the Strugatskys had always fought shy of tying themselves to precise A.D. dates, but from time to time they had dropped them in. From this point on, they start providing only the last two or three digits of the year or other somewhat vague indications. Often a little research or deductive reasoning suffices to provide the exact year or even day of a story, but by their vagueness the Strugatskys are probably asking not to be held too firmly to such dates. As many writers have ruefully testified, it is nearly impossible to attain complete self-consistency in a future history.

Certainly from a thematic viewpoint, and probably also by internal chronology, the next work to consider is the short novel *Far Rainbow* (1964). This takes place in roughly 2190; it is a sort of *Titanic* story in space. The thinly settled planet Rainbow serves primarily as a scientific colony for experiments in interstellar teleportation, which the Strugatskys call "null transport" (or "zero transportation," depending on the translation). As the story opens, the biggest problem is the squabbling over the distribution of the scientific equipment brought in by Gorbovsky, Falkenstein, and Dickson. The equipment shortage, while only temporary and occasioned by Rainbow's isolation, is putting the Marxist ideal of material abundance under severe strain, and is taking its toll on the personalities of the researchers. Then the squabbling is brought to a quick end by the appearance of a deadly black Wave, the accidental by-product of the teleportation research, sweeping down from each pole and dooming all life on Rainbow. The colonists acquit themselves well, both in fighting the Wave, and after they have realized all is lost. Gorbovsky's single ship is the one means of escape, and on it go the colony's children. There is no room for the results of the scientific research which so recently had seemed all-consuming. The ship is piloted by a teenager, for the crew itself has stayed behind. We last see Gorbovsky seconds away from heroic certain death. This time a touch of mysticism is added, not by unhuman aliens, but by the half-human Camill, the last survivor of an experiment in bionics which increased his stamina and his reasoning power, but which cost him much of his ability to feel emotions. Though assured of regeneration once the deadly Wave has passed and killed the others, Camill envies his doomed companions for their ability to have led full lives.

Far Rainbow thus serves as a capstone to one phase of the Strugatskys' work; the material and spiritual triumph of communist man has been shown in its completeness. But this was not to be the end of the future history itself, for the Strugatsky brothers had already demonstrated the ability to look beyond this perfection—to look both farther into the future and back into the past. In "Escape Attempt" (untranslated, 1962), a group of young men out on a vacation jaunt stumble upon Saula, the first discovered planet with near-human inhabitants. Indeed, the near-humans have managed to set up a slave labor system that seems a cross between a Roman *latifundium* and Stalin's Gulag. The well-meaning but naive children of the future try to help but only succeed in making things worse. Other notable features of "Escape Attempt" include a depiction of a Wanderer teleport installation and a fantasy motif, striking in itself, although out of accord with the general science fictional feel of the future history, about a "fugitive" from World War II who finds the courage to go back through time and fire his last round. But it is the larger theme of communist man's intervention in less developed societies which will be carried over into other Strugatsky works.

The increased element of foreboding in Strugatsky work may have been inspired not merely by an exhaustion of the theme of perfection, but because of changes in the contemporary world. By the mid-sixties, many of Khrushchev's grandiose plans had collapsed in failure. Others showed some success, but not enough to fulfill the promise to "overtake and surpass" the West in the near future. Disclosures about the Stalin era and the erection of the Berlin Wall suggested something about the present level of Communist ethics, perhaps making a future blossoming into righteousness seem less plausible. In 1964, Khrushchev himself was ousted and denounced for "hare-brained scheming," and the new Brezhnev leadership showed no real sign of any ambition beyond a preservation of the status quo. In 1967, when the second edition of *Noon: 22nd Century* appeared, the authors found it fitting to add a preface which stated, among other things, that the book depicted the future world the way the authors would like to see it, not as they particularly expected it to be.

In 1965, the year after Brezhnev came to power, the Strugatskys published *The Final Circle of Paradise*. The book is another attack on *meshchanstvo*, as represented by Western hedonism and especially by "the slug," direct stimulation of the brain's pleasure center (what Larry Niven calls "wire-heading"), a device so powerful that it has corrupted the two UN investigators preceding Zhilin. In the depicted struggle against the slug, still in progress when the novel closes, and in new allusions to a European war, which apparently pitted UN forces including both the Soviets and the Americans against "the fascists" in about 2010, the Strugatskys seem to be laying new emphasis on the problems which lie between the present-day world and the one their future history portrays.

It would be four years between the publication of *Final Circle* and the magazine publication of the next future history work (six years to the latter's book publication). The hiatus resulted in part from a change in the Strugatskys' literary interest, and in part from the increased displeasure by which the brothers were viewed by the régime, or at least by one powerful faction within the leadership. On the one hand, the authors seem to have felt an urge to go "beyond" science fiction, and in particular to experiment with surrealism, a movement frowned upon by the régime but enjoying much popularity among "serious" Russian writers. On the other hand, whether because of these new ventures into unapproved literary forms, or because their anti-Stalinist and generally antiauthoritarian themes were becoming too pointed for the tolerance of the régime, the Strugatskys were coming under increased critical attack and finding it increasingly difficult to get published. But when the brothers did return to orthodox science fiction with *Prisoners of Power* (magazine version, 1969; book, 1971), the novel displayed no more political caution than previous books and no diminution of artistic power. *Prisoners* is a swift and colorful adventure novel which also contains much serious discussion of issues of government, ethics, and war and peace.

The hero is young Maxim Kammerer, a German who has joined yet another of those paramilitary scientific organizations, the Free Search Group (also rendered as the "Independent Reconnaissance Unit"), and who finds himself marooned on the uncharted planet Saraksh, a post-nuclear-holocaust world where one of the surviving countries is ruled by an anonymous totalitarian clique, the "Creators."

Maxim is properly horrified at the planet's plight, and he resolves to do what he can to ease it. This pits one person against a world, but Maxim is not without assets. The bionic medical research which produced the unhappy Camill has apparently since been paying off in a more positive fashion. Maxim has prodigious powers of reasoning and memory. He can read, in a foreign language, as fast as he can page through a book, and he devours treatises on higher mathematics for amusement. He can see in the dark, can sense radioactivity without instruments, and he is next to unkillable. Even so, success eludes Maxim as he tries one "career" after another in pursuit of his goal: Pro-régime Legionnaire, underground terrorist, prisoner in a labor camp, agitator attempting to stir up the borderland mutants, convict soldier, and participant in the power games among the Creators. Maxim survives radioactive contamination, bullets, and death camps, but by the climax of the novel, all he has managed to accomplish is to get his best friend killed and to touch off a premature uprising that may end by making matters even worse. Maxim's immediate predicament is eased when it is revealed that a Creator nicknamed Pilgrim is not at all Maxim's greatest enemy, but rather another Earthling, part of a covert operation mounted by the Council for Galactic Security. Maxim has found his rescue, but we are left with an impression of the staggering and thankless task communist Earth has set itself in trying to uplift lesser-developed planets.

Science fiction stories are rarely susceptible to one-to-one mapping onto present-day reality. When they can be so mapped, there is little excuse, save perhaps the incidental one of evasion of censorship, for presenting them as SF in the first place. Still, somewhat more complex analogies frequently exist. On one level, the planet Saraksh is Earth between World Wars I and II, with the geography rotated ninety degrees, from east-to-west to north-to-south. The country ruled by the Creators is Russia ruled by the Communist Party complete with purges and labor camps. The novel's rejection, not necessarily of Marxist-Leninist ideals or even of the Communist Party of the sixties, but of the methods of the Stalin era, seems thorough and vehement, though the practical consequences are less well defined. The Strugatskys repeatedly demonstrate that any attempt to improve matters may instead make them worse, and they even pass on the advice, odd for moralistic writers, that a little flexibility of conscience is not altogether a bad thing.

On another level, Saraksh stands in, not for Earth in the thirties, but for Earth following a nuclear war—in fact, two of them. A global war had been fought about thirty years before, with consequences sufficiently dire even if not quite on the doomsday scale of much Western SF or the one other Soviet after-the-bomb novel, Bulychev's *The Last War*. During the course of *Prisoners*, another war is fought with tactical nuclear weapons and armored forces. This latter level of conflict, while much discussed in both Western and Soviet military theory, has for some reason not been much dealt with even in Western SF. In *Prisoners*, the Creators' invading forces are blown to pieces, which possibly represents a Strugatsky warning against even tactical-level nuclear adventurism.

It would seem that after some initial indecision, the régime concluded that it did not care to listen to such advice. Since the appearance of the book version of *Prisoners* in 1971, the Strugatskys have been placed in one of those nicely calculated gradations of disfavor which the régime manages with such delicacy. The brothers have not been banned, but their publication rate in the seventies dropped drastically from the sixties level. Moreover, while they have placed works in magazines and anthologies (publications with substantial circulations, at that), while some of these works have, with Soviet approval, appeared as books in Eastern Europe and the West, and while one of them has even served as the basis for a Soviet motion picture, the only book with the Strugatsky name on the title page to appear in the USSR in the past decade was a reprint of *Noon: 22nd Century*, with one seventies novella appended. Still, the limited production of the past decade, including the half of it which fits into their future history, has continued to be no less interesting than what went before it.

The first of these is "The Kid" (untranslated, 1971), set in the mid-twenty-third century. The authors allude within the work

to Kipling's *Jungle Book*, but the story would really seem to be
the Strugatsky answer to *Tarzan* or the first part of Heinlein's
Stranger in a Strange Land; the orphan of castaway parents is
raised by nonhumans and in consequence develops unhuman
powers. A new Strugatsky twist, consistent with their general
partiality toward unseen aliens, is that the Kid has never met his
nonhuman benefactors, has not even realized that such must
exist to account for his survival and physiological adaptation to
the hostile environment. One of the major plot conflicts is between those humans who see the Kid only as a bridge to contact
with these mysterious aliens and those who want to protect his
rights as an individual. An additional complication arises when
it is discovered that a Wanderer sentry satellite had shot down
the Kid's parents' ship. Who were the Wanderers trying to guard
from whom? The immediate story problems are resolved by
evacuating the humans to a space station and providing the Kid
with a videophone, so that his human education and very cau-
tious efforts at contact can continue. In the meantime, the reader
has been left with a good deal to ponder, both in the realm of
lofty issues such as the essence of humanness and the ultimate
destiny of intelligent life, and more immediately in terms of
implications for a future history. The Wanderers now seem closer
and more threatening. Here their artifacts are only hundreds of
thousands of years old, not tens of millions as on Mars and Vladislava, and for the first time the Wanderers have more or less
intentionally killed human beings, though a not-too-convincing
explanation is advanced that the robot satellite was intended to
destroy only unmanned probes. Even human society seems less
idyllic. COMCON, the agency regulating contact with nonhumanoid extraterrestrials, proves to have dictatorial legal authority, not surprising given the logic of the situation, but not sitting
very well with the Marxist notion of the replacement of the
"government of persons" by the "administration of things" under
communism. On the more positive side, the Strugatskys blithely
bring Gorbovsky back on stage despite having all but killed him
off in *Far Rainbow*, fifty years or more earlier by internal chronology. Vexingly enough, to this day the authors have not written,
or at least have not published, the story explaining his escape
from an inevitable doom only seconds away. One possibility is

that Gorbovsky did die on Rainbow and the person appearing later is an artificial recreation with the original's memory up to the recording session imposed upon it. A similar recording session was shown in *Noon*, though at that stage the technology for making a new body and brain on which to impose the memory did not yet exist.

Despite the title, "The Fellow from Hell" (1976, untranslated) returns to an optimistic view of life on Earth, as contrasted with underdeveloped hell-planets such as the viewpoint character's native Giganda. Giganda has the approximate technological level of Earth's 1930s and a social structure more like the nineteenth century. Its natives are doing their primitive best to destroy themselves in war. The protagonist, Gahg, is a young "Warcat" in the service of the Duke of Alai. Meanwhile, Terrestrial secret agents strive to stop the fighting and, in the longer run, to promote the planet's transition to communism. A group of them come across Gahg just after he has been burned by a flamethrower and bring him back to Earth for medical treatment and possible recruitment as an agent. However, Kornei, director of the Gigandan operations center in the Russian steppe, finds his attention distracted by fast-breaking events on Giganda. Consequently, Gahg, still loyal to the Duke, is left more or less to his own devices at the operations center. Through his eyes we get a few glimpses of developments on Earth, mostly technological ones such as the widespread introduction of teleportation for local travel and of the Phantom spacecraft for nearly instantaneous interstellar travel. We also get a fairly detailed look—through Gahg's largely uncomprehending eyes—at the management of a covert intervention on an underdeveloped planet. The previous efforts we had witnessed on Saula and Saraksh had not gone particularly smoothly, but it seems that Earth has learned from the experience—and not only Earth, for the Giganda operation is a cooperative one involving humanoids and nonhumanoids from a number of worlds. The plot of the story is a bit thin, as if the novelette were an intended novel hastily brought to a close about halfway through. The Strugatskys give us a good picture of the horrors of war on Giganda and a good psychological portrait of Gahg as a loyal soldier of the Duke, but they do less well with his stirring doubts after his contact with communist society.

The most recent future history work, and its first full novel to appear in a decade (still only in magazine serialization in the USSR) is *Beetle in the Anthill* (1980). The viewpoint character is Maxim Kammerer from *Prisoners of Power*, now twenty-five years older but still working under Rudolf Sikorski, the former "Pilgrim" on Saraksh. The two of them now work on Earth itself on behalf of "COMCON-2." It is not entirely clear whether this organization just uses the original Commission on Contacts (now COMCON-1) as a cover, or whether -2 is an outgrowth of -1, perhaps by way of regulating technology transfer from extraterrestrial civilizations. In any case, by now COMCON-2 has become a police force much like Larry Niven's ARM, with responsibility, among other things, for enforcing the laws restricting dangerous technological innovations, whether imported or invented. Unlike Niven's ARM stories, however, *Beetle* is not modeled on the classical mystery. Instead, it is reminiscent of one of John Le Carré's bleak spy novels.

The convoluted plot centers about Maxim's efforts to track down one Lev Abalkin, a "Progressor" who had been working on Giganda. Abalkin apparently had a mental collapse, may have killed another agent on Giganda, and has returned to Earth and disappeared. Maxim strongly suspects that there is more to it than he is being told, and the investigation itself turns up one puzzle after another. Finally, Maxim's insistence and the pressure of events force the truth out of Sikorski: Abalkin is suspected of being a sort of "sleeper" agent in the service of the Wanderers. He is the product of one of thirteen apparently human fertilized ova that the Wanderers had placed in preservation in another stellar system forty thousand years earlier.

Speculations on the purpose of the cache range from the benign (that the Wanderers have created intermediaries to facilitate contact with the human civilization which they foresaw) to the sinister (that the ova have been "booby-trapped" with genetic programming that will suddenly express itself at some point in the organism's development). Balancing caution against curiosity, the World Council had decided to let the Thirteen grow up in human society, but also to place them under observation and channel them into professions that will keep them away from Earth. Knowledge of their origins has been kept from all but two of the Thirteen. (Of the two who had the news broken to them in adulthood, one took it quite calmly, but the other committed suicide). Thirteen small discs found with the ova and now kept at the Museum of Nonterrestrial Civilizations are linked to the Thirteen by some means beyond the comprehension of contemporary science. Using his skills as a secret agent, Abalkin has apparently found out about his origin and about the existence of the discs and he is trying to get at them. Sikorski, seeing in this the next step in some nefarious Wanderer plot, is determined to stop him at all costs. In the climax, Sikorski shoots Abalkin dead and is convinced he has saved humanity from nameless horrors. Maxim, for his part, is not sure that anything more has happened than that suspicion and fear of the unknown have driven both Sikorski and Abalkin to tragedy.

On one level, then, *Beetle* simply combines the frequent Strugatsky theme of human reaction to mysterious alien intrusion with the theme of a "mutant" misfit conflicting with society. On this level *Beetle* succeeds, particularly in its depictions of Abalkin and his two nearest approximations to friends—Maya Glumova, who also tried to befriend the Kid, and the canoid alien Schokn—and squarely in the Strugatsky tradition. *Beetle* represents a substantial break with past work, however, when we examine what the Strugatskys have done to the social background. In a manner only remotely and weakly anticipated by "The Kid," *Beetle* negates or contradicts much of the spirit of the works that came before it. COMCON-2, in the supposed era of the "administration of things," is nothing less than an organ of state coercion, and at that, one staffed by former covert operatives accustomed to working outside the law. The Assignment Commission which forces young Abalkin against his inclination into an offworld profession is similar to an organization mentioned in Efremov's *Andromeda*, but this is the first hint of such an authoritarian body in the Strugatsky history; even under today's "socialism" nothing like it exists. Further, we are suddenly made aware of a mania for secrecy in the Strugatsky future society, though it faces no external threat save conceivably the superadvanced Wanderers. The only object of this secrecy can be to keep information out of the hands of the public—a public that has enjoyed full communism for two-and-a-half centuries!

Indeed, the single positive new social factor in the novel is the existence of, and official tolerance of, Dr. Bromberg, a sort of Ralph Nader figure. But even Bromberg operates in a "checks-and-balances" role that stems from Western liberalism rather than from the Marxist view of the future that hitherto has shaped Strugatsky works.

Externally, the Strugatsky society is suddenly having severe doubts about the benevolence or even the neutrality of other advanced civilizations. In part this has been justified by changed circumstances. In 2253, Abalkin and Schokn discovered proof that the Wanderers were still active in the galaxy, no longer comfortable millenia away. But *Beetle* reads this fear back into previous times, the 2230s saw not only the deep suspicion about the Thirteen but also the still-secret Operation Mirror, quasi-military maneuvers for the repulsion of a posited Wanderer invasion! If the ten million years that the Wanderers have possessed advanced technology is not enough to have brought them to a benevolent communism, however nonhuman they may be, then the whole of dialectic materialism would seem to be in severe trouble indeed, and with it the assumptions that have governed the Strugatsky future history.

What are we to make of all this? Three possibilities, not necessarily mutually exclusive, suggest themselves. One is that the authors' "sabotaging" of their own future history was unintentional, a manifestation of nothing more profound than sloppy craftsmanship. The authors wanted to tell a story about a misfit abused by society, and with no ulterior motive in mind, they adjusted the details of their future until it became capable of producing the desired abuse. But why use the future history at all for such a story? About half of the authors' recent writing lies outside this projected background. Moreover, the Strugatskys seem to have gone out of their way to make allusions to previous works and to recruit characters from them. They seem anxious to emphasize continuity even as they undermine it.

A second possibility is that the Strugatskys are deliberately putting their future society through a crisis, a theme familiar in Western SF. We can see three forces threatening human society in *Beetle*. All of them stem from technological advance, two of them in particular from the existence of extraterrestial civilizations. One is the psychologically and socially injurious effect on humans of the large-scale covert operations on underdeveloped planets. So long as they continue, Earth cannot really outgrow its precommunist past; yet, paradoxically, if these efforts to help cease, it will mean human society has sunk below communist morality. The second force is the knowledge of the existence of highly advanced extraterrestrial civilizations which might, by some unforeseen quirk, turn out to be hostile or which might threaten humans quite unwittingly. The maintenance of some sort of defense establishment and of military discipline and secrecy may seem a necessary precaution, however much it retards social development. The third force at work is the threefold extension of lifespan, which facilitates the entrenchment of a gerontocracy. Maxim has been working under Sikorski for twenty-five years, and Gorbovsky has been well known for over 150 years and has held high administrative office for at least fifty. Such long tenure hampers the rise of people more in tune with the times and allows problems such as the Thirteen to prey upon the same minds for decade after decade. If the Strugatskys have indeed intentionally depicted a crisis of growth brought on by forces such as these, we can expect future stories to show characters coming more fully to grips with the social problems which are only raised in *Beetle*.

A third hypothesis is that changes in contemporary Soviet society and social thought have finally forced changes in the future history's underlying structure. Émigrés and visitors report that in the USSR today there is wholesale disillusionment with the Marxist-Leninist ideology. This may or may not be an exaggeration, but certainly the optimistic enthusiasm of the Khrushchev era is long past. The Marxist-Leninist utopia at the heart of the Strugatsky future history may be losing all relevance to its readers and indeed to the authors themselves. Still, the Strugatskys would feel a natural reluctance to abandon a background which they have spent so many years building up, to which their imaginations are now attuned, and which holds characters such as Gorbovsky, who evidently compelled his makers to bring him back from the dead. Instead of abandoning the future history, the Strugatskys may be in the process of fitting it in retrospect into something less idealistic and more in keeping with the realities of human nature as they now see them. How far they can go in this retrospection may be a matter for negotiation between the brothers and a censor obliged to defend the accepted forms of the state "religion," empty of belief though these forms may now be. Since the régime is now paying the price in popular disillusionment for the exaggerated expectations aroused under Khrushchev, it might actually welcome a certain toning down of the depicted glories of the communist future.

After these speculations on the fate of the Strugatsky future history in the authors' homeland, we can turn for a moment to the question of the fate of their stories in the United States. The Strugatskys first saw print in 1959, and they were already well in stride as writers at a time when many of today's established American figures were still breaking in. Unfortunately, early Strugatsky translations were of varying quality, and frequently they were Moscow-published, meaning both that the "safest" works were chosen and that the resultant editions were hard to obtain in the U.S. Not until the mid-1970s did truly representative Strugatsky works start to see reasonable distribution in this country. Had circumstances permitted quicker translations, American readers already would have known of Wanderer artifacts when they first examined the relics of Niven's Slaver Empire; they would have wandered across Saraksh with Maxim Kammerer at about the same time as they journeyed over Le Guin's Gethen with Genly Ai, and they would have recalled *Noon: 22nd Century* when they came to *The Dispossessed*. Timely translation plus the inherent quality of the Strugatsky work would have assured the brothers of an influential role in the sixties. By now American science fiction has duplicated or moved past many of the early Strugatsky innovations, while at the same time much of the brothers' more recent work has moved to an East European set of conventions less likely to catch on in the U.S. But science fiction readers have always shown themselves ready to cherish the best work of past decades. The time for maximum influence on other writers may have been missed, but now that most of the Strugatsky future history works are available in English, the series can take its place alongside Niven's Known Space, Anderson's Technic Civilization, or Le Guin's Hainish series as one of the major products of the past quarter-century of science fiction.

9

Carolyn Wendell

RESPONSIBLE REBELLION IN VONDA N. McINTYRE'S *FIREFLOOD, DREAMSNAKE,* AND *EXILE WAITING*

Vonda McIntyre has been publishing science fiction since she was in college, majoring in genetics. She continued writing science fiction while working on a doctorate in genetics, then realized that "as a scientist, I was a pretty good science fiction writer. I sort of crept off, before any of my professors noticed that, too." The professors' loss has been the readers' gain. Her output has been less than prolific in the last decade ("I write very slowly; I work on lots of research, think about it and mull it over," she explains; then she rewrites extensively). Nevertheless, although she has written only a handful of short stories, two novellas, and three novels (the latest, a "Star Trek" novel, *The Entropy Effect,* will not be discussed here), she has won two Nebulas (one for the short story, "Of Mist, and Grass, and Sand," which became the opening chapter for her Nebula award-winning novel, *Dreamsnake*) and been nominated for a third ("Aztecs").

In addition to her own fiction, McIntyre is known for having coedited, along with Susan Janice Anderson, *Aurora: Beyond Equality,* a feminist anthology of stories set in nonsexist societies. Her own work is, at first glance, feminist. With only a few exceptions, her central characters are strong, independent, assertive females who play conventionally male roles—sneak thief and rebel (Mischa, in *The Exile Waiting*); prisoner in a labor camp (Kylis, in "Screwtop"); space pilot (Laenea, in "Aztecs"); prison escapee (Dark, in "Fireflood"); doctor or healer (Snake, in *Dreamsnake*). Males in these stories play, at best, secondary roles or, at worst, are portrayed as brutes and weaklings. This becomes particularly obvious, even distracting, at times. In *Dreamsnake*, for example, there are few males in important positions; the guards, horsebreeders, prospectors, innkeepers, and elders are all women. The mayor of Mountainside, selfish and insensitive, is a man; the "crazy" is a man; North, the deformed and psychotic villain, is a man; Ras, the brutal child-molester, is a man. The gentle and persistent Arevin is neither brutal nor weak—nor is he in very much of the story.

In the same novel, McIntyre also consciously plays with gender preconceptions. Frequently the reader is introduced to a woman with a typically male job; for example, Snake goes to a chemist in Mountainside for more aspirin and iodine. She enters and the woman who runs the shop is referred to as "the proprietor" and "the chemist" before the pronoun "she" is used. An even more extreme example, because longer sustained, occurs in Snake's encounter with the dying Jesse (who is a woman, although her name has the masculine spelling) and her partners, Alex (male, in name and pronoun) and Merideth ("Meredeth" is a male name, but the spelling has been slightly changed here), who is never identified by pronoun, so the character could be either male or female. While this technique is hardly original (for example, P. J. Plauger used it in "Here Be Dragons" in *Aurora: Beyond Equality*), it does present a feminist lesson: one's gender is less important than one's personality and capabilities.

McIntyre, in interviews, clearly sees herself as a feminist and credits Joanna Russ for her raised consciousness. McIntyre's first story was published under "V. N. McIntyre"; when she told Russ this at the Clarion SF Writers Workship in the late 60s, Russ said, "Don't do it any more." She has not, and admits that "it was very important to me, around the age of twenty, to be told that I was a human being, even though I was a girl."

And her feminist feeling that people are human beings, regardless of gender, shapes her own fiction:

"If I wanted to write about a sexist society, I'd write mainstream. I don't see any point for anyone who is a feminist or humanist or anything like that to reconstruct the problems of our society in science fiction. I think that's a waste of science fiction. I think a lot of writers reconstruct our society in science fiction because they're comfortable with present day life. I'm not. I'm interested in change, in other possibilities."

In fact, a careful investigation of McIntyre's fiction reveals a concern with issues not exclusively female, but pervasively human: imprisonment that wastes human potential and a movement to freedom that allows, even requires, a sense of responsibility for the self and others. Women, in particular, have become aware in the last decade-and-a-half of the social and psychological traps laid for them, but, as McIntyre points out, "The feminist movement is not just about rights, it's about responsibilities." In her stories, both male and female characters learn about freedom (rights) and responsibility as they move— or try to move—from imprisonment to freedom and responsibility. Some succeed, others do not.

The causes of enslavement in McIntyre's fiction fall into at least three overlapping categories: human oppressors, physical reasons (appearance, disease, old age, etc.) and self-imposed psychological manacles (often a misplaced sense of obligation to family members).

Most obviously, slaves abound in McIntyre's two major novels. The Stone Palace of Center, the setting of *The Exile Waiting*, is filled with slaves—mostly the providers of their masters' or mistresses' sexual pleasure. Captured young and thoroughly trained, they know little else. Saita, Blaise's slave, accompanies him constantly, wearing little and saying less, ready to please him at all times. Subone, who angrily regards slavery as an illogical waste of human potential, asks her how long she has been in the Stone Palace, and she answers, "The Lady Clarissa has said three years, Lord." She knows nothing but the giving of sexual pleasure, probably not even how to read a calendar and gauge the passage of time in her own life. In the last chapter, when the outcasts from the underground have seized the Palace, Saita and her equivalent, Lady Clarissa's boy slave, are told they are free, but neither of them understands what that means or, if they do, it is a terrifying idea, for the boy breaks into "despairing tears." So then, the final horror of slavery is that the victim may become used to it.

On the other hand, Madame, one of McIntyre's most fascinating characters, has retained her dignity even as a slave, never emotionally accepting her situation. She is too unattractive to be used sexually, but she is intelligent and forceful enough to be a very efficient Palace steward, a position she has held for years. She conducts herself with an icy calm, sealing herself off from the world around her (Mischa, who is telepathic, cannot sense her at all: Madame was "self-contained, guarded, opaque.") She does not ever obviously rebel against her masters, but Subtwo notices her annoying manner of responding only to:

> . . .questions asked, not questions implied. It was a small defiance that could neither be identified nor objected to on any level of rationality. This similarity of a human being to a computer might have pleased him some time before, but now, with this human being, it did not.

She even responds to her freedom with the same control, calmly removing the slave ring from her finger and surrendering her whip, noting that she never used it. She thinks how she is "Madame" no longer (we never do learn her real name—slavery removes identity), "and the knowledge was the sunlight she had not seen since she was eight years old." However, whether Madame will ever be a fully functional, feeling human being is debatable. She and Subtwo hold hands on the flight from earth, both like children, according to Jan's journal. Perhaps nearly a lifetime of slavery, of repressing one's self, can be overcome, but a child has only to learn, whereas Madame must unlearn. She is both the most admirable and the most pitiable of McIntyre's slaves.

In *Dreamsnake*, Snake meets freed slaves, Brian and Larrill, at the mayor's residence in Mountainside. Although the mayor is portrayed as a selfish and almost thoroughly unpleasant character, he did, years before, outlaw slavery in his town. Both Brian and Larrill were freed by that law, but they still bear the scars.

Larrill's is the visible one—rings in her heels. Snake tells her that they might be surgically removed, but only at the risk of a crippling limp. But even that threat cannot temper Larrill's joy that the symbols of her former state might be removed. Brian bears no visible signs of his slavery, but his gratitude to the mayor, has, unhappily, resulted in his own voluntary enslavement as the mayor's servant, at his imperious beck and call every minute. Snake disapproves, but little can be done to free a willing slave.

Those stories in which human oppressors enslave both the body and the spirit, with no hope for successful rebellion, are some of McIntyre's most poignant. "Spectra," for example, deals with a youngster (no clue as to gender and no name) who is treated as a machine by his/her captors. The narrator's eyes have been removed so that he/she can be fitted with a helmet and perform incomprehensible tasks for his/her captors: the mechanical apparatus of the helmet allows the prisoner to perceive patterns of light and dark while his/her hands work controls as instructed. The narrator sleeps in a coffin-like box where "cannulae" feed into a valve implanted in his/her ankle. Although the others around the narrator are similarly imprisoned, they do not mind; they even enjoy the patterns their helmets allow them to see. But the narrator recalls seeing, recalls being captured and removed from his/her mother, and suffers anguish because he/she wants his/her eyes back. "Spectra" (presumably a reference to the colors the narrator can no longer see) offers a human being in perhaps the worst trap of all: no identity, no vision, and, in short, merely a substitute for a machine, with no hope of ever being free, human.

"The End's Beginning" is narrated by a dolphin, also unidentified by name or gender. It has been captured by human beings and surgically implanted with a detonation device. Like the narrator of "Spectra," it recalls its previous, free life and agonizes its loss, but it is also aware of the final horror its captors and tormentors will inflict on the whole world, killing both themselves and "all the people" (the dolphins). This, the narrator thinks, is "the end's beginning." As in *A Canticle for Leibowitz*, only the shark will remain when all else is dead.

"Elfreda" also offers a poignant comment on human use of

others. The mythical creatures of the story were human once, but chose physical transformation over death and are now centaurs, nymphs, and merfolk. Their human masters created them with little respect for them or for mythic truth: these artificially created nymphs are male while the artificial satyrs are female. There are various sizes of pegasoi, but only the smaller ones can fly; "it would not occur to them [the human creators] that a flying horse's heart might break because she could not fly." The humans make regular appearances to participate in sex orgies with their creatures. Their one free creation is Elfreda, a unicorn who is too swift for them to capture, until this time, when she is trapped and led off if in ropes. The narrator, a centaur who loved her and tried to help her, breaks his leg and will be shot.

Kylis, in the novella "Screwtop" is also a prisoner, but in a more conventional sense than the characters in the already-mentioned stories. She is a spaceport rat—a stowaway on starships and in spaceports—who was arrested and sentenced to prison, and now confined to Screwtop, a work camp where prisoners dig wells to provide the planet Redsun with geothermal energy under conditions that almost guarantee injury and death. The place sounds like a concentration camp or hell itself: the arrival of prisoners jammed into small compartments where some have died; unremitting heat and humidity; a pall of smoke and ash from burned vegetation; impenetrable boundaries of volcanoes and marsh; a guard captain, cold and uncaring except for his own desires, always dressed in black, nicknamed the Lizard. Ironically, there is hope for Kylis although she has no chance of physical escape, because she has retained—and fights to keep—her spirit. Her captors succeed only in confining her body, and that for a limited time (until the end of her prison term). Kylis is spared psychological destruction by her proud sense of responsibility for others. It is suggested that this is a recent change in her; before coming to Redsun, she had just begun to wonder if there were more to life than outwitting spaceport security guards. She is amazed to find herself, after a life of "complete independence and self-sufficiency" caring for other people. We see only the results of this personality change, not the process. Kylis first takes Gryf, a political prisoner, under her wing, then Jason, weaker than she and Gryf and in greater need of protection. The three form a loving and mutually supportive partnership or family.

By the end of the novella, Kylis has stood up to the Lizard, who wanted her to bear a child which she would then surrender to him. Primarily because she is unwilling to surrender any human being, particularly a helpless child, over to "this dreadful, crippled person," she has succeeded in refusing him, regardless of his temptations and threats (his similarity to the devil is obvious here). She has also been instrumental in attaining Gryf's release and obtaining the chance for Jason to be ransomed by his family. Kylis turns from the plane taking Gryf away into the "gentle light of dawn" while "the harsh spotlights dimmed one by one." The more positive imagery of these last sentences points out the positive development of the story. Although the central character is not yet physically free, she has retained her dignity and her humanity by helping those she loves and refusing to bend to tyranny. There should be little doubt that eventually she will be completely free.

Dark, the protagonist of "Fireflood," is also a prisoner, but less like Kylis and more like those in "The End's Beginning" and "Elfreda." She and others in the story volunteered to be biologically changed into physical specimens capable of colonizing alien worlds. But the colonization project has been scrapped, leaving the experimental subjects confined to reservations. Dark is a digger, equipped with claws, armored body, and transmuted senses so that she can live deep below the surface of a planet (the underside of a deadly volcano seems stimulating and beautiful to her). The flyers are former human beings now capable of graceful flight. Dark escapes from her reservation and makes her way to the flyers' reservation where she asks them to join the diggers in pressuring the human beings to reinstate the original project, so that both diggers and flyers can be released from their useless captivity. The flyers will not help, though, and at the end, Dark is dragged off by human captors.

Dark and the flyers are not only confined to reservations (prison), but they are also trapped by their physical bodies, which make purposeful lives impossible. On yet another level, Dark suffers yet one more form of what Blake called "mind-forged manacles"—she is ugly. Jay, the flyer, explains that he and his kind would need to go through another stage of transformation before being ready to colonize; after that, they would not be able to fly on earth—and the flyers fear being stranded on this planet where they would never be able to fly again. Dark angrily responds, "What troubles you is that when you were finished, you wouldn't be beautiful anymore. You'd be ugly like me." Jay does not deny her accusation. And, indeed, the flyers are admired, almost worshipped, by their human masters while the diggers are despised.

This particular handicap of ugliness appears occasionally in McIntyre's stories, and it can be argued that this is a feminist concern. Physical beauty garners greater social acceptance and thus more benefits and freedoms than does homeliness. All people are equal, but pretty girls are more equal than plain ones, and blondes have more fun. Women are made quire aware of this from infancy, and we see it reflected in McIntyre's fiction.

In *Dreamsnake*, for instance, Melissa is trapped, not only by the guardianship of the brutal Ras, but by her badly-scarred face. The people of Mountainside are both healthy and beautiful (perhaps illogically, given the long-term effects of radiation and a small gene pool), so Melissa must be the child who may be heard but cannot be seen. She has learned to hide when she can and when she cannot, to hold her head so that her hair covers the scarred side of her face. The only time Snake becomes angry at Gabriel, a gentle and kind man, is when he sees Melissa's face and involuntarily flinches, and Snake realizes Melissa's ugliness will never be tolerated by the townspeople. When the mayor later comments that perhaps Ras has not been unkind in hiding the girl, Snake snaps, "All you people see is beauty," even though she realizes they do not understand what she means. That these false standards for judgment exist in society is reemphasized when Snake goes to Center where she is greeted with, "I'd think they could choose somebody handsome." Snake ignores his comment, merely realizing that his tone is one of insult. Ugliness can be a socially-forged manacle, too. Snake's ignoring the remark shows that her society (different from both Mountainside and our own) does not regard appearance as a way to judge people.

Some of McIntyre's characters are less free than they could be because of their appearance; others also suffer because of their abnormalities. Society is quick to single out and ostracize those who are different, in appearance, in ability, in age. Rebellion and freedom are possible, but improbable.

In "Only at Night," deformed, retarded children are watched over by a nurse who is more than a bit intimidated by her charges, who finally rebel and knock her to the floor—or did she dream it? She fantasizes herself crucified by them, wearing a crown of needles and catheters, but not rising in three days. The villain in this short but disturbing story seems to be the parents who have "spawned monsters that they're afraid to love. They're perfect people who hide their mistakes." The narrator debates whether to return to her job after her experience and concludes that, if she does, she will return to the night shift again because the parents visit only in the daytime. Imprisonment can result from rejection as well as from capture. The story also seems to suggest that human hatred of flaws may stem from fears about the imperfect self.

Retardation and deformity can make one an alien from society; so can old age. Two of McIntyre's stories deal with the flyers of "Fireflood" and handle the stigma of old age.

The world has been deserted by the flyers in "Wings." Still left is the keeper of a temple long since abandoned by its god. And the keeper is old and crippled by a badly healed wing, which he broke when he fell after accompanying his aged mate in her death ritual. Young flyers are neuter until they mate with an older flyer, when they take on characteristics of that sex opposite their mate's (McIntyre's admiration for Le Guin is evident here as we recall the similar sex choice made by Gethenians when they come into kemmer in *The Left Hand of Darkness*). An old flyer chooses the time of death, flying higher and higher until life is no longer viable. Usually he/she is accompanied by the younger mate who carries veils which the younger tucks into the elder's finger- and ankle-bands. The keeper, though, is alone until he rescues and cares for a young flyer, still neuter and apparently left behind by the other flyers, possibly because his eyes are too light in color to have allowed him to fly very high. The keeper is attracted to the youth, but will not force himself

upon the youngster, who is bitter and cynical about the abandoned world. The youth finally heals and leaves. When he returns a year later, having confirmed his suspicions of a deserted
world, the keeper is near death and asks the youth to carry his
veils. The youth promises to build the crippled flyer a glider so
that he may die in the air.

A spaceship carrying the flyers who had left the world behind
is the setting for "The Mountains of Sunset, the Mountains of
Dawn." Again, there is an old flyer, female, and a young one, as
yet neuter. The old one dreams of her youth, flying "high enough
to see the earth's curvature" and of her dead eldermate. On board
ship for many years, the flyers have accepted constraints that
only the old one still rebels against—the cramped space that
limits flying, meat animals whose taste is bland. She grudgingly
accepts her imprisonment until the ship reaches a planet; then,
when the others decide the gravity is too heavy, she leaves the
ship. A youth who loves her follows her, they mate, and when
his change is complete, he accompanies her on her death ritual;
although she cannot fly "high enough for cosmic rays to burst
against her retinas," she "took comfort in the clear sky and in
flying." She dies as she had wanted.

Both these flyer stories offer a pathos dependent upon an imprisonment of the old by circumstances, which leave them
strangers in a world they did not make. The key to this prison
is death, and both aged flyers are fortunate to find youths who
care enough to help them make the transition. Death, for them,
is freedom.

The knowledge of imminent death, as an escape from life's
prison, can also be a stimulus to emotional growth and caring.
"The Genius Freaks" is one of McIntyre's most powerful stories,
a fresh approach to the overdone science fiction theme of su-
perchildren. Lais is a fifteen-year-old genius, genetically engineered by "the Institute." She had been aware even in her artificial womb and felt imprisoned by its cramped darkness. Birth
propelled her into a larger prison—the Institute administrators
care only about "sucking up the last fruits of her mind and all
the information her body could give them." The world outside
rebels against "freaks" (this is suggested, but not delineated in
any great detail). Even worse, normal people have lifespans of

150 years while Institute Fellows have only 30 years—and, in Lais's case, only half of that.

The story begins after Lais has fled the Institute, is experiencing great pain, and realizes she is near death. Her freedom from the Institute and her awareness of her desperate state forces her to a reliance on, and kindness to, others that she has never felt (or needed to). An old and pathetic man allows her to sleep in his room, and she realizes that she is able to treat him with a gentleness that would have been alien to her when she had still been at the Institute: "she would have looked on him not with compassion but with the kind of impersonal pity that is almost disdain." Later, she is able to acquire access to a computer—not only does she not use her ability to disrupt the city, even though she sees many ways to do that, she places into storage her discovery that a cancer virus may have been brought into a cancer-free society. Her own extreme plight teaches her a human responsibility she had not felt before. Lais disappears into the jungle surrounding the city as "the sky was changing from midnight blue to gray and scarlet with the dawn." Like the end of "Screwtop," imagery stresses the growth of character.

The most memorable examples of isolation because of differences are the underground people in *The Exile Waiting*. Generations of in-breeding and radiation-damaged genes have caused abnormalities that range from slight (Val has a pelt of red hair) to severe (Crab is barely recognizable as human and his thoughts are so jumbled he can communicate only with Mischa). Center has followed, probably for generations, a tradition of abandoning in the deeper caves infants born with visible deformities (those like Mischa, whose telepathy cannot be seen, are safe). The pathetically deprived conditions under which the underground people live while caring for one another with great compassion contrast dramatically with the luxurious conditions of Stone Palace with its callous and cruel inhabitants. The underground people do succeed in rebellion, however, and the novel ends on a note of hope that the rebels will bring freedom and comfort to the above-ground slaves.

One last character falls under this category of isolation and imprisonment because of physical state: Laenea in "Aztecs." In order to become a pilot, Laenea has had her heart removed and a mechanical pump transplanted into her chest; for reasons not fully explained in the story, natural human rhythms cannot adjust to periods of "transit" time on a spaceship, so the crew must sleep through those periods while the pilots must have their natural hearts removed. When Laenea meets her former peers, the crew members, she senses something has changed: she finally leaves them, deciding that she "would not taunt them with her freedom." That last word becomes horribly ironic as the story develops. Laenea feels smug, superior, and arrogant about her new status. No longer does she have to sleep through transit: she is a pilot and will see it all, as only a pilot can, for transit cannot be described and pilots will not even try. Laenea knows there is a convention that pilot and crew do not mix, but she, in her new superiority, attributes this to superstition and snobbery, so when she meets a new crewman, Radu Dracul, she falls in love with him and he with her. But every time they make love, her body responds too rapidly, and afterwards she loses her finely honed biocontrol over her physical system, each time taking longer to regain it. Meanwhile, Radu has nightmares that are far too real, and that they both fear will kill him. The two finally realize they must part: their two biological rhythms, hers artificial and his natural, cannot be made to mesh. And Laenea goes to join the pilots, "to live apart with them and never tell their secrets."

The story's title is partially explained within the story: a slang term for pilots is "Aztecs." When a stranger calls Laenea this, she snaps, "The Aztecs sacrificed their captives' hearts. . . . We don't feel we've made a sacrifice." Radu Dracul is clearly evocative of Dracula lore (a fact Laenea comments on when she meets him), particularly when we learn he is from the planet Twilight. Laenea was partially right: she is not an Aztec, but she is a sacrificial victim, and Radu would have been her innocent killer, draining the life from her, as well as her unknowing victim, dying himself. Laenea gave up her heart to obtain something she wanted, but she ironically has had to surrender the love she also wants. She is free to be a pilot, but barred from Radu forever.

The two areas discussed thus far have been external constraints upon freedom, the manacles forged by others or by the character's physical self that they can do little about. A third perhaps more significant area is that of psychological slavery. The mind-forged manacles are self-produced and willingly worn, unless the victim can learn enough to discard them. These manacles are often those of misplaced responsibility to others, often family members. The characters in McIntyre's two major novels, *The Exile Waiting* and *Dreamsnake*, must free themselves before they can grow to full humanity—a caring relationship with others.

The Exile Waiting, McIntyre's first novel, involves several characters, most of whom are imprisoned in various kinds of cages. The slaves have already been discussed, and certainly Madame can serve as a touchstone for slavery: she wears the outward signs of submission but has maintained her dignity. The underground people discussed earlier, imprisoned by their society's fear of their genetic abnormalities, manage to survive, though not very well, until Mischa's actions offer them the opportunity to escape. Like most of the major characters in the novel, Val, the leader of the underground people, is where she is because of her own family. It was her own cousins that spotted her deformity, her own relatives that tied her down until the pulled-out hair grew back to prove her less than human. Mischa realizes that is the real bitterness in her, and the real fear: "the memory of being exposed and displayed as an animal." Finally she faces the cousin who had exposed her when her people take over the palace; by then we have seen her as the careful and caring leader of others, and when she tells Madame that Saita "can still grow, with the rest of us" we believe her, since she speaks from her own experience.

The three major characters, Subtwo, Jan Hikaru, and Mischa, are all entangled with their obligations to their families. Each is struggling at the start of the novel to find his/her own identity, his/her own life. Because each is so entrapped, each is an "exile waiting"—for his/her own actions to break the bonds.

It takes the whole novel for Subtwo to break free of his ties, his sense of responsibility for his pseudosibling. The two of them, "the behavioral equivalents of genetic twins" were biomechanically linked, apparently resulting in a kind of telepathy. They "should have been free of one another long before," but the link still functions. Subtwo struggles to be an independent human being who feels like other human beings (that he falls in love with Madame points out both his potential and their similarity). Subone is all Subtwo is not: brutish, violent, sensually decadent, and manipulative. Subtwo's pursuit of Mischa and Jan through the underground caverns seems to be, symbolically, his death and descent to the underworld from which he emerges naked (symbolically reborn) and able to repudiate his bestial other self. His last moment of rational debate, whether to once more sacrifice himself and others for Subone's benefit, comes (while Subone's teeth glint "bright as a beast's") as Mischa explodes, "He owns you more than he could own any slave. He owns your soul," and Madame stumbles in, injured from Subone's earlier attack on her. Subtwo feels a "great wrench of betrayal," strikes his pseudosib, then concludes, "he had done an impossible, perhaps unforgivable, but necessary thing." "Necessary" is the key word—Subtwo has had to take violent action (the only time he does so in the whole novel) to free himself. Now he can continue to learn what it means to be a human being.

Jan Hikaru also must free himself from a family member: more conventionally than Subtwo, Jan has a domineering father to place in perspective. The son ran away from the father who wanted him to be what he could not, but by the end of the novel, Jan has given Subtwo instructions to take himself and Mischa to his home planet. He tells us in his journal, "Ichiri can't direct my life anymore—he never could, but that I let him. Knowing that, I think I can accept him as he is." Jan's growth to maturity and freedom has been steadier and less dramatic than Subtwo's, but no less painful. His love for the blind poet teaches him the emotional reward of having someone dependent on him (we can fairly assume he had known only the receiving end in his relationship with his father). Ichiri Hikaru had wanted Jan to participate in a literary fantasy he had created; the blind poet dreams of dying on earth—Jan helps her do this, even lying to her as she dies, describing an earth that used to be, not the one he sees. This may well teach him a lesson applicable to his father: fantasies are not necessarily harmful; in fact, they may defend and protect.

Just as importantly, Jan has dealt with two other experiences all human beings must grapple with if they are to grow up: pain and death. His trek with Mischa through the underground forces him to a courage he had never had before. His fall into the crystal garbage dump nearly kills him, and he recovers only to learn from Mischa that there is nothing left of the personality after death (after which, be expresses homesickness for the first time). Two chapters later, they reach the final resting place of Center's dead. Jan at first gags and falls, but then "he knelt, breathing heavily, drawing the products of corruption into his lungs, accepting, knowing that he was their past, as they were his future."

And, as Jan learns that no one can direct one's life but one's self, so he teaches Mischa, who is even more imprisoned than Jan, on a number of levels. She was born into a poor family, of parents who did not care for their children. This puts her at the bottom rung of her rigidly-structured class society from the start. That she was born telepathic in a society which fears mutation means she must hide what should be a beneficial gift. But that she has a family that use and abuse her is her most confining restriction. Since her parents lived in some fantasy world, oblivious to their children (most of whom were retarded), Mischa's older brother Chris brought her up, giving her an inflexible sense of gratitude and obligation. And perhaps Chris had originally been worthy of her devotion—they shared a telepathic link, he was a talented artist, and the brother and sister formed a defensive team against the world, planning how to escape their planet to Sphere (the colonized worlds). But by the time we meet him, he is a drug addict, his talent ruined by his destroyed senses, out of touch with reality and barely able to function. Worse, when Mischa tries to help him, Chris is abusive and even cruel to her. But because of her sense of indebtedness, Mischa keeps trying to rescue him from one situation after another. As he is dying, he tries to apologize, but Mischa cuts him off: "That was the honor between them, that they were, finally, responsible only for themselves." The falsity of this is made clear by everything that has happened: Chris, pitiful remnant that he is, has caused trouble for Mischa since the very beginning of the novel because she has felt responsible for him and he is clearly unable to care for himself. Only his death finally frees her from this burden. Her link with Chris, like Subtwo's with Subone, is finally broken, and she can act freely.

Mischa also suffers guilt for Jan as well as Chris, but it is Jan who insists that each person is responsible only for himself: "people are responsible for their own decisions, and no one else's." Later it is Mischa who points out to Subtwo that one person making decisions for another all the time is not right.

Mischa's other family manacle that must be broken is her telepathic link with Gemmi, her retarded younger sister who can call Mischa to her whenever their greedy uncle threatens her. Gemmi's handicap makes her the enslaved victim of her uncle (she even wears a chain on her ankle that fastens her to the wall). Her telepathic gift makes Mischa the slave of both sister and uncle, as Gemmi's insistent call can cause Mischa pain and near-insanity. Once Crab, the abandoned and forgotten brother, cuts this link, Mischa is free of Gemmi, and both are free of their brutal and grasping uncle.

Ironically, but fittingly, once Mischa is free and under no compulsion to go to her uncle and Gemmi, she does return there to take Gemmi away. Simon, Val's partner and lover, picks up Gemmi and her dangling chain, and says, in one of the most moving moments of the book, "We will free her. She is one of us." Both themes of the novel, freedom and responsibility, are brought together here.

Dreamsnake, McIntyre's Nebula award-winning novel, utilizes the same themes, but in a very different structure. *The Exile Waiting* deals with only one overall plot, Mischa's attempt to escape Center. While there are numerous subplots involving a variety of characters, all are intertwined (rather like the strands of the DNA helix, so important to the story because of the mutated underground people and because Center itself is described as being constructed in a helix shape). *Dreamsnake* is not quite so complexly structured; in fact, at first it seems to be a picaresque novel whose central character moves from episode to episode. When she leaves the characters of one episode, they do not reappear later (in *The Exile Waiting*, all characters continue from beginning to end). Although Snake has a main purpose in her travels, the quest for a dreamsnake, it is difficult to see the novel as a unified whole unless it is seen in terms of the categories already established in this essay for McIntyre's characters. This application allows us to see a tighter structure than is at first apparent.

And *Dreamsnake* does delineate characters who are imprisoned on various levels. As mentioned earlier, Brian and Larrill are freed slaves who still suffer the effects of their past bonding. Melissa, also discussed earlier, is trapped both by her guardian Ras and by her scars, a physical condition that her community will never tolerate.

Other characters are similarly fettered. It is made clear that the people of Center are imprisoned when Snake goes to Center, which has every ten years been a source of hope for the healers' station when envoys have been sent there to request dreamsnakes (from this, we can deduce that Snake's age is somewhere between 17, her age their last trip, and 27, the timing for the next trip). Attention is drawn to both the size of the gate (five times Snake's height) and its construction, with "no handle, no bell-pull, no door knocker." When Snake learns that the gate is locked until spring, with no way for either insider or outsider to open it, we realize that Center's citizens are locked in as surely as Snake is locked out. Then, when Snake is summarily and angrily dismissed because of her reference to cloning (at which moment the gatekeeper sees Melissa's scarred face), we know it is more than metal gates that confine Center's people. Their own minds forge the manacles that prevent a consideration of genetic manipulation to prevent mutants.

North, the nightmarish villain of the piece, would seem an example of unmotivated evil if it were not for his physical deformity that has caused his psychotic rage at a world that could not cure his albino giantism and undoubtedly would not accept him. Snake tells him that healers might have been able to help him if he had been brought to them as a child, but now it is too late. Defensively—and maniacally—he screams, "Do you think that I want to keep hearing that I *could* have been ordinary?" Because he has been imprisoned within a deformed body, he in turn imprisons those around him, his followers whom he addicts to dreamsnake venom. A "crazy" who pursues Snake is the only one we meet, but his addiction is so strong that he will do and promise anything to procure more venom. Both he and North are permanently imprisoned.

Gabriel, the beautiful son of Mountainside's mayor, is a prisoner in his town and scorned by his own father because of an erroneous biocontrol instruction that had resulted in a pregnancy and dangerous abortion for his younger friend. When Snake asks him about Melissa's hiding for four years, he admits, "I've been hiding from everyone for three years. I guess it's possible." The most painful part of his predicament is his relationship with his father, who is so ashamed of him that he can barely be civil to his son and willingly strikes a bargain that will banish Gabriel from his sight and knowledge forever. As in *The Exile Waiting*, family members, who should be most supportive, instead cause the most pain for their victims. It is Snake who convinces Gabriel that he is not the cripple he believes he is, that there are bio-control methods that can work for him. With him, her role as healer becomes one of guide, teacher, counselor, and lover. She finally tells Gabriel before they part, "Go out in the world. Take your life in your hands and make it what you want," a lesson that could apply to many of McIntyre's characters.

Arevin is told much the same thing by his cousin and leader of his clan. He longs to follow Snake, whom he is attracted to, but whom he also feels responsible for, as he thinks her teachers will never understand his people's fear of snakes that resulted in Grass's death. However, he, like Gabriel, feels responsibility to his family and stays with his family group to care for his cousin's newborn (in a scene which has strongly feminist roots: a man nurturing an infant as lovingly as any woman could). When the leader discovers his tangled feelings, she tells him,

> We do things the way we do them so we can all be as free as possible most of the time, instead of only some of us being free all the time. You're enslaving yourself to responsibility when extraordinary circumstances demand freedom.

Arevin's clan is structured so that responsibility is shared among all members (even for parenting, by way of extended family groups, another sign of McIntyre's feminism): "any of us might be leader, and any of us might have feared the little serpent enough to kill it." Her advice to Arevin, which reveals much about the workings of this particular community, is reminiscent of Le Guin's *The Left Hand of Darkness* where, on Gethen, "Burden and privilege are shared out pretty equally: everybody has the same risk to run or choice to make."

Arevin is relieved in his own mind of the family responsibility so that he may, as Snake has told Gabriel, go out and make his life what he wants it to be: in short, to make his own choices and decisions. He chooses responsibility and caring for Snake, whom he follows on a long, arduous trip. His sporadic appearances in the novel as he moves after Snake troubled many reviewers of the novel when it first appeared as an unnecessary plot twist. In fact, this is simply a feminist reversal of a standard pattern in adventure fiction where the hero is pursued—or worse, is waited for at home—by his female love who does not see him again until the end of the novel when all the excitement is over. The reviewers may have been bothered by the notion of a woman having all the adventures and solving all the problems while the man merely follows her trail and misses all the fun. Even when Arevin does find Snake, he does not rescue her because she has already rescued herself; and then she revives Melissa on her own while Arevin offers what a partner of either gender should—comfort and emotional support. He is not expected to take charge, and he does not.

Snake is called "healer" and healer she is as she aids one person after another, bringing relief from pain (Stavin, Jesse, the mayor and unnamed others) and freedom from the fetters imposed by external forces (Gabriel and Melissa). That she is able to do all this results from the fact that Snake is less imprisoned and more free than any of McIntyre's characters. Snake is slave to no one and manacled by very little. Even when North tries to trap her, she is able to escape both the death he planned for her and the pit itself (her strength seems to come both from her confidence in her own abilities and her responsibility to keep her promises to Melissa). Nor does she suffer the tyranny of physical handicap, although her experimentation with immunities has left her with an arthritic knee, she is physically strong. Nor is she so unattractive that society—even the physically perfect citizens of Mountainside—tries to isolate her. Nor is she fettered by a sense of misplaced obligation to family. Rather, her extended, adoptive family at the healers' station thinks highly of her (as evidenced by their giving her her name, which is seldom given, and then only to those who are highly regarded). Even when Arevin reports to them her loss of Grass and he is disappointed that they do not immediately forgive her, they do not condemn her or show anything but concern. They simply want her to come home.

Because Snake is free, she can make choices—and her choice is responsibility. Wherever she goes, she changes lives for the better through her own conscious efforts. Her quest for a dream-snake is part of her freely-made choice. When she makes that decision after she leaves Jesse's camp, we are told that she "had been raised to be proud and self-reliant," and to return to her home would be to sacrifice those qualities. Although Snake faces obstacles (some of which are of her own making, like her fears of being arrogant), the life that she leads is a product of freely-chosen responsibility.

Snake is the kind of person most of McIntyre's characters are not, but might be, if the restrictions that imprison them could be removed. Snake is the kind of person we could wish there were more of in the world outside of fiction: free to choose responsibility and caring for others.

Notes

PAGE	QUOTE	SOURCE

1. Reaching for Immortality (Krulik)

1	"Both of these movies"	Damon Knight, *In Search of Wonder* (Chicago, Illinois: Advent Publishers, 1967), p. 278.
3	"He stared a while"	Richard Matheson, *The Shrinking Man* (New York: Bantam Books, 1969), p. 63.
4	"You cannot take away"	James H. Burns, "Richard Matheson on 'The Honorable Tradition of Writing,' " *The Twilight Zone Magazine*, vol. 1, no. 6 (September, 1981), p. 46.
4	"He has a profound"	*In Search of Wonder*, p. 239.
6	"just that amount"	*The Shrinking Man*, p. 102.
8	"Poets and philosophers"	Ibid., p. 35.
9	"he'd never be small"	Ibid., p. 84.
9	"It was not a man's"	Ibid., p. 89.
9	"The authority of"	Ibid., pp. 175–176.
10	"It would be a"	Ibid., p. 7.
10	"Why go through all"	Richard Matheson, *I Am Legend* (New York: Berkley Medallion, 1971), p. 26.
10	"I'll kill every"	Ibid., p. 27.
10	"I was too used to"	Ibid., p. 169.
10	"In spite of having"	Ibid., p. 168.

PAGE	QUOTE	SOURCE
10	"Like death, his fate"	*The Shrinking Man*, p. 51.
11	"All the coincidences"	Ibid., p. 184.
11	"He didn't let himself"	Ibid., p. 126.
12	"He could sleep without"	Ibid., p. 165.
12	"Bacteria can mutate."	*I Am Legend*, p. 157.
12	"Robert Neville looked"	Ibid., pp. 173–174.
13	"He looked up"	*The Shrinking Man*, p. 187.
13	"To nature there was"	Ibid., p. 188.

SELECTED BIBLIOGRAPHY

Burns, James H. "Richard Matheson on 'The Honorable Tradition of Writing,' " *The Twilight Zone Magazine*, vol. 1, number 6 (September, 1981), 43–50.

Knight, Damon. *In Search of Wonder*. Chicago, Illinois: Advent Publishers, 1967.

Matheson, Richard. *I Am Legend*. New York: Berkley Medallion, 1971.

———. *The Shrinking Man*. New York: Bantam Books, 1969.

Nicholls, Peter. *The Science Fiction Encyclopedia*. New York: Dolphin Books, 1979.

2. Hero As Hedonist (Salmonson)

19	"rather wade"	Doris Piserchia, *Mister Justice* (New York: Ace Books, 1975), p. 24.

SELECTED BIBLIOGRAPHY

Piserchia, Doris. *The Billion Days of Earth*. New York: Bantam, 1976.

———. *Earth Child*. New York: DAW Books, 1977.

———. *Mister Justice*. New York: Ace Books, 1975.

———. *Spaceling*. New York: DAW Books, 1979.

———. *Star Rider*. New York: Bantam Books, 1974.

Vance, Jack. *The Dying Earth*. Underwood/Miller, 1977.

———. *The Eyes of the Underworld*. Underwood/Miller, 1977.

3. The Rhetoric of Science in Fiction (Rabkin)

24	"we trust the arts"	Earl Miner, "Literature as Knowledge," *Critical Inquiry* (Spring, 1976).
26	"It is only the very"	Samuel Butler, *Erewhon* (1872), ch. 20.

PAGE	QUOTE	SOURCE
27	"The weather"	Ibid., ch. 3.
28	"There are and can"	Francis Bacon, *Novum Organum* (1620).
29	"All these things"	Sir Isaac Newton, *Opticks* (1704).
30	"The wish to"	Arthur C. Clarke, *The View From Serendip* (New York: Random House, 1977), p. 192.
32	"A new scientific"	Max Planck, *Scientific Autobiography* (1949).
33	David A. Kronick	"Authorship and Authority in the Scientific Periodicals of the Seventeenth and Eighteenth Centuries," *The Library Journal* (July, 1978).
34	"Ideally the general"	John Ziman, *Reliable Knowledge* (1978), ch. 1.
35	Jeremy Warburg	"Poetry and Industrialism," *Modern Language Review* (April, 1958).
36	"Alone among the"	Herbert L. Sussman, *Victorians and the Machine* (1968), ch. 2.
36	"Schoolmaster Gradgrind"	Charles Dickens, *Hard Times* (1854).
36	"Thomas Gradgrind, sir"	Ibid.
37	"Today we can see"	Alan J. Friedman, "Contemporary American Physics Fiction," *American Journal of Physics* (May, 1979).
37	"They say farther"	Francis Bacon, *The New Atlantis* (1627).
37	"When I asked"	Cyrano de Bergerac, *Other Worlds* (1657), ch. 20.
38	"the observation"	*American Heritage Dictionary.*
39	"Since you are"	Voltaire, *Micromegas* (1752), ch. 7.
40	"the gentleman"	Ibid., ch. 3.
40	Darko Suvin	*Metamorphoses of Science Fiction* (1979), ch. 7.
40	"A left-handed shell!"	Jules Verne, *Twenty Thousand Leagues Under the Sea* (1869), ch. 22.
40	"They're classified"	Ibid., ch. 14.
41	"Apparently the age"	Arthur Conan Doyle, *The Lost World* (1912), ch. 16.

4. Ian Watson's Miracle Men (Chauvin)

45   "The point is"   Ian Watson, *Vector* 78 (November–December, 1976), p. 8.

45   "The basic plan"   Ian Watson, *The Embedding* (New York: Scribner's, 1973), p. 45.

46   "all the children"   Ibid., p. 19.

46   "Christ no!"   Ibid., p. 43.

46   "*Nouvelles Impressions*"   "Raymond Roussel and his poem are real. Roussel was born in 1877, and the *Nouvelles Impressions d'Afrique*, a volume whose title harks back to his prose *Impressions* . . . , came out first complete in 1932. Its four sections total 1,276 lines, including those 286½ that are printed as long verse footnotes, and each section (one has 644 lines) incorporates immense parentheses within parentheses, the major ones being enclosed within successively one, two . . . five brackets, thus [[[[[. Roussel would actually have preferred the use of different coloured inks. Cutting across all this, and looping remorselessly into footnotes and up again, the line-structure is one of common alexandrine couplets. The syntax of phrases is more or less conventional (unlike some of Mallarmé). Generally the first argument, soon relinquished, in each of the great four sections, has to wait till nearly the end to be resumed. . . . The poem can only be 'read' by backtracking on the pages, i.e., it is primarily visual, plus perhaps long-term articulatory memory where mental cues can be attached. The question has to arise, whether any merely auditory-articulatory short term memory mechanism could cope (no matter

PAGE	QUOTE	SOURCE

how brain-development were stimulated) with actual discourse so introvoluted and elephantine."

—David I. Masson, review of *The Embedding, Foundation* 5 (January, 1974), pp. 81–82.

47   "The Change Speakers"   *The Embedding*, p. 158.

47   "possess a common"   Ian Watson, *Vector* 71 (December, 1975), p. 16.

47   "if the structure"   Ibid., p. 16.

48   "The fabric of space"   Ian Watson, *The Jonah Kit* (New York: Scribner's, 1975), p. 71.

48   "You are in effect"   Ibid., p. 95.

48   "a Universe is quite"   Ian Watson, *Vector* 71 (December, 1975), pp. 18–19.

50   "Yet we still live"   *The Jonah Kit*, p. 210.

50   "Japan was the big"   Ian Watson, *Vector* 86 (March–April, 1978), p. 7.

50   "two Japanese concepts"   Nigel Sellars, *Seldon's Plan* 47 (December, 1980), pp. 21–22.

50   "uneasy co-existence"   Ian Watson, *The Martian Inca*, (London: Panther, 1977), p. 60.

50   "They [the Indians] were"   Ibid., pp. 71–72.

51   "All I really saw"   Ibid., p. 109.

51   "Mutations aren't just"   Ibid., p. 162.

52   "How does living"   Ian Watson, *Vector* 71 (December, 1975) p. 20.

52   David Wingrove   *Vector* 86 (March–April, 1978), pp. 12–16.

52   "We are in the sort"   Ian Watson, "W(h)ither SF?", *Vector* 78 (November–December, 1976), p. 11.

52   "out of one model"   *The Martian Inca*, p. 164.

53   "universally recognized"   Quoted by James Blish in "The Science in Science Fiction," *Vector* 69 (Summer, 1975), p. 7.

53   "the most important"   Ibid., p. 10.

53   "Living creatures"   Ian Watson, *Miracle Visitors* (New York: Ace Books, 1978), p. 53.

PAGE	QUOTE	SOURCE
54	"A voice hooted"	Ibid., p. 129.
54	"You cannot grasp"	Ibid., p. 196.
54	"We couldn't tolerate"	Ibid., p. 197.
55	"often brought help"	Ibid., p. 81.
55	"Our way"	Ibid., p. 174.
55	"The Phenomenon"	Ibid., p. 225.
56	"Why not a phantom"	Ibid., p. 250.
56	"The universe, he"	Ibid., p. 267.
57	"When you investigate"	Ibid., p. 281.
57	"There are no casual"	Ibid., p. 293.
57	"How did one define"	Ibid., p. 299.
58	"The map stretched"	Ibid., p. 334.
58	"You are an enigma"	Ibid., p. 334.
58	"suggests the possibility"	Brian Stableford, *Foundation* 16 (May, 1979), p. 67.
58	"as he tells an"	James Blish, *The Issue At Hand* (Chicago: Advent Publishers, 1964), p. 6.

RELATED READINGS

Watson, Ian. *Alien Embassy*. London: Victor Gollancz, 1977.

———. *God's World*. London: Victor Gollancz, 1980. (Published only in England.)

———. *The Very Slow Time Machine*. London: Victor Gollancz, 1978.

NONFICTION:

Watson, Ian. "Toward An Alien Linguistics," *Vector* 71 (December, 1975).

———. "W(h)ither SF?" *Vector* 78 (November–December, 1976).

(*Vector* is the official journal of the British Science Fiction Association.)

5. Science at the Crossroads (Hassler)

63	"Bones was fascinated"	Hal Clement, *The Nitrogen Fix* (New York: Ace Books, 1980), pp. 208–209.
67	"You people all"	Hal Clement, "Impediment," *Natives of Space* (New York: Ballantine Books, 1965), pp. 153–54.
70	"You know as well"	Hal Clement, *Star Light* (New York: Ballantine Books, 1971), p. 224.
72	"I have not been"	*The Nitrogen Fix*, p. 272.

6. Roger Zelazny's Bold New Mythologies (Yoke)

74   "Zelazny's stories are"   Theodore Sturgeon, "Introduction," *Four for Tomorrow*, by Roger Zelazny (New York: Ace Books, 1973), p. 8–9.

75   "Job's wealth and status"   Job 1:3.

75   "sore boils from"   Ibid., 1:18–19.

76   "Ikky is a symbol"   Calvin S. Hall and Vernon J. Nordby, *A Primer of Jungian Psychology* (New York: New American Library, 1973), pp. 48–49. For an interesting discussion of the leviathan archetype, see Northrop Frye's *Anatomy of Criticism*, Third Essay, "Archetypal Criticism: Theory of Myths," pp. 189–192 in the 1973 paperback edition.

76   "Hephaestus myths"   John Pinset, *Greek Mythology* (London: The Hamlyn Publishing Group, 1973), p. 39.

77   "The earth thus"   Pierre Grimal, ed., *Larousse World Mythology* (London: The Hamlyn Publishing Group, 1969), p. 130.

77   "Thus, sacrifices are"   Ibid., p. 534.

77   "the Priapus of"   W. B. Seabrook, *The Magic Island* (New York: Harcourt, Brace, and Company, 1929), p. 290.

77   "Other signs of wonder"   Ibid., p. 65.

78   "The Devil is"   Jeffrey Burton Russell, *The Devil: Perceptions of Evil from Antiquity to Primitive Christianity* (Ithaca, N.Y.: Cornell University Press, 1977). p. 126.

80   "Fenris actually"   Snorri Sturluson, *The Prose Edda*, trans. by Arthur Gilchrest Brodeur (London: Oxford University Press, 1916), p. 78.

81   "to restore to Hinduism"   Joseph Politella, *Seven Religions* (Kent, Ohio: Kent State University Press, 1958), p. 66.

PAGE	QUOTE	SOURCE
81	"the tyrannical"	Ibid., p. 66.
82	"Chaos appears"	*The Devil: Perceptions of Evil*, p. 67.
82	"a pure white animal"	Odell Shephard, *The Lore of the Unicorn* (New York: Barnes & Noble, 1967), pp. 71, 81.
82	"The unicorn"	Ibid., pp. 150–154.
83	"King of the Grail"	Ibid., p. 82.
83	"red-haired people"	*The Devil: Perceptions of Evil*, fn. 14, p. 66.
83	"The reddish glow"	Ibid., p. 64.
84	"the lore of the Tarot"	Eden Gray, *A Complete Guide to the Tarot* (New York: Crown Publishers, 1970), p. 150.
84	"Devil is the polar"	Ibid., p. 37.
84	"Archangel is"	Ibid., p. 36.
84	"Caine, yet another"	Roger Zelazny, *The Courts of Chaos* (New York: Doubleday and Company, 1978), p. 151.
84	"Ganelon explains to"	Roger Zelazny, *The Guns of Avalon* (New York: Doubleday and Company, 1972), p. 33.
86	"Osirus, Tammuz, Adonis"	Sir James G. Frazer, *The New Golden Bough* (New York: Criterion Books, 1959), pp. 284–285.
87	"an old aboriginal"	Erwin Rhode, *Psyche: The Cult of Souls and Belief in Immortality Among the Greeks* (Freeport, NY.: Books for Libraries Press, 1972), p. 321.
87	"Conrad plays the"	*The New Golden Bough*, p. 317.
87	"Conrad is Greek'	Ibid., p. 362.
87	"Conrad's sanctuary is"	Ibid., p. 362.
87	"In her investigations"	Jessie L. Weston, *From Ritual to Romance* (Garden City, N.Y.: Doubleday and Company, 1957), p. 48.
88	"by which we"	Mark Schorer, "The Necessity of Myth," *Myth and Mythmaking*, ed. Henry A. Murray (Boston: Beacon Press, 1959), p. 355.

PAGE	QUOTE	SOURCE
88	"fundamental, the dramatic"	Ibid., p. 356.
88	"I somewhat subscribe"	Roger Zelazny, "Unpublished Letter" (August 29, 1971).

7. Four Voices in Robert Silverberg's *Dying Inside* (Alterman)

92	"Poor goofy Yeats"	Robert Silverberg, *Dying Inside* (New York: Scribners, 1972), p. 2.
92	"The two books"	Ibid., p. 23.
92	"It's always been"	Ibid., p. 30.
93	"myself and . . . that"	Ibid., p. 1.
93	"society's ugliest"	Ibid., p. 17.
93	"why I always"	Ibid., p. 104.
93	"the problem is"	Ibid., p. 113.
94	"Where's my identity?"	Ibid., p. 89.
94	"behind this merely"	Ibid., p. 182.
94	"let nothing"	Ibid., p. 164.
94	"They'd all love me"	Ibid., p. 238.
94	"Yes! Oh, the"	Ibid., p. 230.
95	"the real stuff"	Ibid., p. 19.
95	"Human beings, says"	Ibid., pp. 203–204.
96	"A roaring furnace"	Ibid., p. 72.
96	"Europydes Sophocles"	Ibid., p. 72.
97	"Her love is"	Ibid., pp. 32–33.
97	"all the years"	Ibid., p. 91.
97	"We're locked in"	Ibid., p. 92.
98	"I embrace her"	Ibid., p. 238.
98	"As the power"	Ibid., pp. 125–126.
99	"who simply sinks"	Ibid., p. 24.
100	"What the hell"	Ibid., p. 151.

8. Future History, Soviet Style (McGuire)

107	"Chinese"	In the mid-1960s, after the Sino-Soviet split, China became an "un-nation," lower than even the capitalist world and unfit for mention. From this point on, in continuing allusions

PAGE	QUOTE	SOURCE

and in revisions of older stories, all Chinese characters are given new nationalities, usually Japanese. Only the circumlunar space station Chi-Fei (from the Chinese for "takeoff") seems to have escaped the censor's notice.

107   "next two stories"   *Shest' spichek* (Six Matches), a collection of short stories, at least some of which were intended to be in the future history, also appeared in 1960. However, some of these stories were reworked into the revised *Noon: 22nd Century*, while others were declared "uncanonical" because they are contradicted by later, more substantial works. Accordingly, *Shest' spichek* will not be discussed here. Similarly, unless otherwise specified, references in the text are to the revised (1967) version of *Noon*, which was the basis for the English translation.

108   "Heinlein Individuals"   Alexei Panshin, *Heinlein in Dimension* (Chicago: Advent, 1968), pp. 129–30.

110   "USCR instead of USSR"   In the original, SSKR for SSSR.

114   "Escape Attempt"   Reference is made in the story to Julian Day 2,542,967, which would place it in A.D. 2249. Such a dating is inconsistent with later stories. Something like 2210 might be more appropriate.

114   near-human inhabitants   While, say, Edgar Rice Burroughs could populate Mars with more or less human beings without blinking an eyelash, contemporary Western authors wishing to indulge in such practices have felt obliged to rationalize, either by positing that Earth

PAGE   QUOTE   SOURCE

and other planets had been seeded
by alien colonizers, or by setting the
story in the far future and making
Earth itself the colonizer. Since Soviet censorship guidelines more or
less rule out social retrogression on
"lost colonies" and an extraterrestrial
origin for human life on Earth, the
Strugatskys have been forced back to
the position of depicting "humanoids" frequently indistinguishable
from humans without offering more
of a rationalization than a few vague
noises about parallel evolution. Since
the Strugatskys draw no clear critical
distinction between science fiction
and fantasy, the situation bothers
them less than it might many Western
writers. For further discussion of censorship guidelines for Soviet SF see
Patrick Llewellyn McGuire, *Red
Stars: Political Aspects of Soviet Science Fiction*, Ph.D. dissertation,
Princeton University, 1977 (available
from University Microfilms International), and sources cited there.

114 "other Strugatsky works"   One of the best developments of the
theme lies outside the future history
(though in a setting that differs in no
major respects) in *Hard to Be a God*
(1964).

116 "a Creator nicknamed   For unfathomable reasons, the nick-
     Pilgrim"   name remains in Russian, *Strannik*,
in the English translation. *Strannik*
can also be rendered as "Wanderer."

116 "east-to-west to"   The English translation somewhat
obscures this relation by placing the
Island Empire in the Arctic instead
of the proper Antarctic. See p. 64 of
the English translation and *Obitae-*

myi ostrov (Moscow: Detskaia literatura, 1971), p. 75.

120   "Rudolf Sikorski"   But Pilgrim's first and middle names had been given as Karl Ludwig in an allusion in "The Kid" ("Malysh," *Polden', XXII vek. Malysh* [Moscow: Detskaia literatura, 1975], p. 440). This is only one of several minor discrepancies suggesting that the Strugatskys would have done well to reread "The Kid" before sending off *Beetle.*

120   "one took it quite"   This individual turns out to be Kornei from "Fellow." However, Kornei's selection for this role seems to have been a rather poorly conceived afterthought on the authors' part, since Kornei knew his father ("Paren' iz preispodnei," *Nezrimyi most,* ed. Evg. Brandis [Leningrad: Detskaia literatura, 1976], p. 191) and has a son of his own. *Beetle* tells us that the Thirteen were placed in nurseries with the cover story that they were orphans and raised in boarding schools (not adopted); and surely if there is fear of "booby-trapped" genes, either the Thirteen would not be allowed to reproduce, or else the offspring would be kept under the same observation as the parents, of which *Beetle* makes no mention. Once again this lapse appears to be a consequence of the long gap between future history stories and of the authors' apparent failure to review previous work before adding to the series.

121   "the canoid alien"   Schokn is a Golovan (from the Russian for "Bighead"), a member of a species on Saraksh that had been

more intelligent than dogs to begin
with, and which then mutated to full
reason after the nuclear war. Maxim
had a brief encounter with them in
Prisoners of Power, but Schokn is the
Strugatskys's first close-up portrait of
a nonhumanoid extraterrestrial, and
he is successful enough to make the
reader wish the authors had made the
attempt years earlier.

SELECTED BIBLIOGRAPHY

In this essay, works are referred to by the title of the English translation
where one exists, and otherwise by a translation of the Russian title.
The most up-to-date bibliography of Strugatsky titles in Russian can be
found in Darko Suvin's introduction to the Strugatskys' fantasy *The
Snail on the Slope* (New York: Bantam, 1980), pp. 2–3. In the same
article Suvin touches on the Strugatsky future history, a theme mostly
ignored by Soviet critics, perhaps because the future history construction is less familiar to them than to Westerners. Adol'f Urban, *Fantastika
i nash mir* (Leningrad: Sovetskii pisatel', 1972) does provide (pp.
162–211) a good discussion of early Strugatsky work, chiefly stories
fitting into the future history. Urban is less successful with the more recent
titles he examines. Below is a listing, roughly in internal chron-
ological order, of the English translations of the major future history
titles. The standard Library of Congress forms of the authors' names are
Strugatskii, Arkadii Natonovich and Strugatskii, Boris Natonovich. The
most common variant transliterations of the surname are Strugatski and
Strugatsky.

Strugatsky, Arkady and Boris. "Destination Amaltheia," trans. Leonid
Kolesnikov, in *Destination: Amaltheia*, ed. Richard Dixon. Moscow:
Foreign Languages Publishing House, n.d. (Note the misspelling of
the moon Amalthea.)
_____ . *Space Apprentice*, trans. Antonina W. Bouis. New York: Mac-
millan, 1981.
_____ . *The Final Circle of Paradise*, trans. Leonid Renen. New York:
DAW, 1976.
_____ . *Noon: 22nd Century*, trans. Patrick L. McGuire. New York:
Macmillan, 1978.

_____ . *Far Rainbow*, trans. A. G. Myers. Moscow: Mir, 1967; also "Far Rainbow," trans. Antonina W. Bouis, in *Far Rainbow/The Second Invasion from Mars*. New York: Macmillan, 1979.

_____ . *Prisoners of Power*, trans. Helen Saltz Jacobson. New York: Macmillan, 1977.

_____ . *Beetle in the Anthill*, trans. Antonina W. Bouis. New York: Macmillan, 1980.

9. Responsible Rebellion in Vonda M. McIntyre (Wendell)

125	"as a scientist"	Ed Naha, "Vonda McIntyre," *Future Life* (September, 1979), p. 24.
125	"I write very slowly"	Geraldine Morse, "Interview: Vonda McIntyre," *Galileo* (November, 1979), p. 11.
126	"Don't do it any more"	Ibid., p. 9.
127	"If I wanted to write"	Naha, p. 24.
127	"The feminist movement"	Paul Novitski, "*Starship* Interview: Vonda N. McIntyre," *Starship* (Spring, 1979), p. 21.
127	"The Lady Clarissa"	Vonda N. McIntyre, *The Exile Waiting* (Garden City, New York: Nelson Doubleday, Inc., 1975), ch. 6.
128	"self-contained"	Ibid., ch. 3.
128	"questions asked"	Ibid., ch. 8.
128	"and the knowledge"	Ibid., ch. 16.
129	"might be removed"	Vonda N. McIntyre, *Dreamsnake* (Boston: Houghton Mifflin Company, 1978), ch. 6.
130	"it would not occur to"	Vonda N. McIntyre, "Elfreda," *New Dimensions 12*, ed. Marta Randall and Robert Silverberg (New York: Pocket Books, 1981), p. 90.
130	"complete independence"	Vonda N. McIntyre, "Screwtop," *Fireflood and Other Stories* (Boston: Houghton Mifflin Company, 1979), p. 94.
131	"this dreadful"	Ibid., p. 128.
131	"gentle light of dawn"	Ibid., p. 145.
132	"What troubles you"	Vonda N. McIntyre, "Fireflood," *Fireflood and Other Stories* (Boston:

PAGE	QUOTE	SOURCE
		Houghton Mifflin Company, 1979), p. 18.
132	"The only time"	*Dreamsnake*, ch. 7.
132	"All you people"	Ibid., ch. 8.
132	"I'd think they"	Ibid., ch. 9.
133	"spawned monsters"	Vonda N. McIntyre, "Only at Night," *Fireflood and Other Stories* (Boston: Houghton Mifflin Company, 1979), p. 148.
134	"high enough"	Vonda N. McIntyre, "The Mountains of Sunset, the Mountains of Dawn," *Fireflood and Other Stories* (Boston: Houghton Mifflin Company, 1979), p. 71.
134	"took comfort"	Ibid., p. 83.
134	"sucking up the last"	Vonda N. McIntyre, "The Genius Freaks," *Fireflood and Other Stories* (Boston: Houghton Mifflin Company, 1979), p. 174.
135	"she would have"	Ibid., p. 178.
135	"the sky was changing"	Ibid., p. 186.
136	"would not taunt"	Vonda N. McIntyre, "Aztecs," *Fireflood and Other Stories* (Boston: Houghton Mifflin Company, 1979), p. 199.
136	"to live apart with"	Ibid., p. 244.
136	"The Aztecs sacrificed"	Ibid., p. 214.
137	"The memory of"	*The Exile Waiting*, ch. 13.
137	"can still grow"	Ibid., ch. 16.
137	"the behavioral"	Ibid., ch. 6.
137	"should have been"	Ibid., ch. 4.
138	"bright as a beast's"	Ibid., ch. 16.
138	"Ichiri can't direct"	Ibid., ch. 16.
138	"Ichiri Hikaru had"	Ibid., ch. 8.
139	"after which, he"	Ibid., ch. 12.
139	"he knelt"	Ibid., ch. 14.
139	"That was the honor"	Ibid., ch. 12.
140	"people are"	Ibid., ch. 11.
140	"Mischa who points"	Ibid., ch. 15.
140	"We will free"	Ibid., ch. 15.

160 Notes

PAGE	QUOTE	SOURCE
141	"no handle, no"	*Dreamsnake*, ch. 9.
141	"Do you think"	Ibid., ch. 11.
142	"I've been hiding"	Ibid., ch. 7.
142	"Go out in the"	Ibid., ch. 8.
142	"We do things"	Ibid., ch. 4.
142	"any of us might"	Ibid., ch. 4.
142	"Burden and privilege"	Ursula K. LeGuin, *The Left Hand of Darkness* (New York: Ace Books, 1969), p. 93. This similarity was mentioned in an unpublished paper delivered by Betsy P. Harfst (Kishwaukee College, Malta, Illinois 60150) at the Science Fiction Research Association Conference, Denver, June, 1981.
144	"had been raised"	*Dreamsnake*, ch. 3.

SELECTED BIBLIOGRAPHY

McIntyre, Vonda N. *Dreamsnake*. Boston: Houghton Mifflin Company, 1978.

———. *The Exile Waiting*. Garden City, New York: Nelson Doubleday, Inc., 1975.

———. *Fireflood and Other Stories*. Boston: Houghton Mifflin Company, 1979.

Morse, Geraldine. "Interview: Vonda McIntyre," *Galileo* (November, 1979), p. 8–11.

Naha, Ed. "Vonda McIntyre," *Future Life* (September, 1979), pp. 24, 56.

Novitski, Paul. "*Starship* Interview: Vonda N. McIntyre," *Starship* (Spring, 1979), pp. 21–28.

About the Contributors

PETER S. ALTERMAN formerly worked for the U.S. Office of Education. He has a Ph.D. in SF and English Romanticism and has written about SF in *Ursula K. Le Guin* (Taplinger, 1979). His short stories have appeared in *New Dimensions Nine* (Harper & Row, 1979, edited by Robert Silverberg) and *2076: The American Tricentennial* (Pyramid, 1977, edited by Edward Bryant).

CY CHAUVIN has been active in SF fandom for years, publishing his own fanzines and appearing on panels at conventions. A technical writer for a manufacturing magazine in Detroit, he edited *A Multitude of Visions*, a small press collection of articles reprinted from fanzines.

DONALD M. HASSLER wrote the book *Erasmus Darwin* (Twayne, 1973) and has published articles in *Science-Fiction Studies, Extrapolation,* and *Great Writers of the English Language* (St. Martin's, 1979). He is active in the Science Fiction Research Association.

TED KRULIK has taught SF in New York City high schools for over nine years. George Elrick's *Science Fiction Handbook* credits him with coining the term "fishbowl effect" (by which SF readers are suddenly exposed to new ideas, as a fish removed from a fishbowl is exposed to a new environment).

PATRICK L. McGUIRE contributed an essay in *The Book of Poul Anderson* (DAW Books, 1975) and an article in the magazine *Galileo,* and one in *Starship.* He was translator for the American edition of *Noon: 22nd Century* by the Strugatsky brothers and was author of the section "Russian SF" in *Anatomy of Wonder* (Bowker, 1981, edited by Neil Barron).

ERIC S. RABKIN is the author of such books as *The Fantastic in Literature* (Princeton, 1976) and *Fantastic Worlds: Myths, Tales, and Stories* (Oxford, 1979) and coauthor with Robert Scholes of *Science Fiction: History, Science, Vision* (Oxford, 1977), considered by many to be the standard historical introduction to SF. He is Professor of English and Associate Dean for Long Range Planning at the University of Michigan.

JESSICA AMANDA SALMONSON has written a series of novels set in an alternate world's Japan, beginning with *Tomoe Gozen* (Ace Books, 1981). Her stories have appeared in *The Berkley Showcase, Amazing Stories,* and elsewhere. In 1980 she won the World Fantasy Award as editor of *Amazons!* (DAW Books, 1979), a story collection featuring women in heroic roles.

CAROLYN WENDELL contributed an article in *Teaching Science Fiction: Education for Tomorrow* (Owlswick Press, 1980, edited by Jack Williamson). Her *Reader's Guide to Alfred Bester* is forthcoming from Starmont.

CARL YOKE is Assistant to the Vice President at Kent State University and has served as Associate Editor of the SF journal *Extrapolation.* He has known Roger Zelazny since the year they shared a desk together in the first grade. Yoke's *Reader's Guide to Roger Zelazny* was published in 1979 by Starmont.

About the Editor

TOM STAICAR is book review columnist for *Amazing Stories* and is the Science Fiction Book Selector for the University of Michigan's Hatcher Graduate Library. He has written articles and reviews published in *Fantastic Stories, Writer's Digest, Science Fiction Review,* and other magazines. Staicar is a member of the Science Fiction Research Association and the SF Oral History Association.

HAVE YOU READ THE ORIGINAL
CRITICAL ENCOUNTERS

Edited by Dick Riley